FALLING FLESH JUST AHEAD

And Other Signs on the Road Toward Midlife

LEE POTTS

LONGSTREET
Atlanta, Georgia

9/28/99
Dear Ellen,
Even though you [illegible] have a chan[illegible] enter-ing the "falling flesh danger zone," I hope you get a laugh out of this.
Best wishes -
Lee Potts

Published by LONGSTREET PRESS, INC.,
a subsidiary of Cox Newspapers,
a subsidiary of Cox Enterprises, Inc.
2140 Newmarket Parkway
Suite 122
Marietta, Georgia 30067

Printed in the United States of America

1st printing, 1998

Library of Congress Catalog Number 97-76263

ISBN: 1-56352-471-6

Jacket design by Burtch Bennett Hunter
Book design by Jill Dible

To Billy
For simply everything

— Acknowledgments —

I would like to acknowledge the help and support of the following people: My sister Sam, who instead of telling me to stand in front of a speeding locomotive to ease my depression about aging, suggested I write a book; my patient, indulgent, surpassingly good-natured husband, Bill, for so freely letting me mine his life for material; Lynne Alpern, tangent decipherer extraordinaire, for decisively pronouncing, "This can work"; my agent Sheree Bykofsky for "totally getting it," taking a chance, and being the consummate professional; Janet Rosen at Sheree Bykofsky Associates for editing prowess and attention to detail beyond the call of duty; John Yow, my most genial and gifted editor at Longstreet Press, for allowing me to tickle his funny bone and for knowing a good made-up word when he hears one; all the friends and family who encouraged me to do it (as well as those who didn't — their skepticism was just the push I needed!); and finally, thanks to God for supplying good timing, synchronicity, and endless grace. Maybe he does know what he's doing after all.

— Contents —

— Introduction —

THE CRISIS DEFINED

Maybe it was seeing the close-up of Keith Richards' face — I apologize if you're eating — on the giant video screen behind the stage at the Rolling Stones concert last year. Maybe it was finding out that the snotty little brat I used to babysit, the one who insisted that people in Amsterdam spoke "Hollandaise" and who thought "Jewish" was a country, is now a producer with an international news organization. Maybe it actually started some years earlier, the first time my husband and I were on vacation with friends, and we realized that nobody's parents were there to pick up the dinner tab. *We* were the parents. *We* were the adults of record. And *we* were expected to pay for the six Cap'n Bob Seafood Samplers, two Landlubber Delites and one highly suspect Catch O' The Day, plus the 20 percent gratuity automatically added for parties of more than eight.

A combination of these and other similar defining moments added up to the horrifying conclusion that I have done what I purposed never to do — aged. I have gotten old. I have lost the glow of youth. Well, I haven't completely lost it. It's just that now it comes out of a bottle and is specially formulated for over-thirty skin. Okay, over-thirty-five. Okay, already, near-forty.

I was born in the middle of the baby boom, and I can tell you that our generation's unprecedented deification of youth has made the passing of that youth seem particularly shocking and harsh. Hey, we really meant it when we said it would never happen to us. At least, I did. Just the other day my doctor cited my advancing years as an explanation for some of my deteriorating parts. "That's what happens as people age," he said matter-of-factly. I wanted to scream, "Yes, Mr. Big Shot Expert, I'm sure it does happen to *people*, but not me personally! Are you blind? Can't you see that I am not people? And what about all that 'age is a state of mind' business? Does Deepak Chopra know you're talking to me like this? I think not!"

Accepting this latest life passage is harder for me because I did not see it coming. I naively thought that because I had suffered a painfully protracted premidlife crisis, I would escape the actual dreaded midlife crisis. My premidlife crisis was nasty. I came of age in the '70s where I was "bright, witty and vulnerable" and served ripe brie at parties. By the mid-'80s I found myself in possession not of the tremendous fame, fortune and flawless skin that were my birthright, but rather of a waylaid career, a marriage and a child, with the accompanying stretch marks. (Accordion pleats is more like it. We're talking Jiffy Pop here.) This was upsetting to someone who used to wear matching underwear ensembles — on weekdays! — and who by 1988 had sunken to having her very own account with the Home Shopping Club. I mean, think about it. I had twenty-four-hour access to vermeil. It was a scary time. But I managed to pull myself out of that nosedive (of course, I can't say enough good things about electroshock therapy) and continued to look forward to each day being the first day of the rest of my life, a philosophy that coincided nicely with what was left of my post-therapy memory.

And now here I am, several years later, enmeshed in yet another personal crisis. Today is not the first "first" day of the rest of my life. I know full well there were many such days that came before, and the longing to retrieve a few of them is overwhelming. The gravitational pull of the past on my heart is strong enough to alter the orbit of a small planet. It seems a minute-by-minute struggle to keep the wistfulness that is never more than one sad, old song away — it should be illegal to carry a concealed Dan Fogelburg album — from overtaking my fragile psyche and plunging me deep into the pit of nostalgia. To a time when mood rings ruled and Clearasil was the drug of choice. Please, I want to go back. I want to do it all over again. The regrets are more than I can bear. (Although to be perfectly honest, 1970s or not, I *deserve* to feel regret over what, judging from my prom picture, was clearly a dangerous and unregulated use of blue eye shadow.)

But my pleas for mercy fall on deaf ears because there simply is no going back. And my cries of protest ring hollow because in my heart I know the truth; I am crossing the threshold into middle age. But don't expect me to cross quietly. I have decided to deal with this unfortunate twist of events in the same self-indulgent way that my generation deals with everything — by talking about it. (Although the judicious use of pharmaceuticals should not be totally ruled out.) We talk about everything. Never mind that some things are better left unsaid. Like the time a woman spontaneously shared with me her painful battle with unwanted back hair while I was standing in line at Eckerd's. I could have gone my whole life without knowing that. I went home and showered. With Clorox.

Unnaturally hairy women aside, I believe talking can be therapeutic. And perhaps opening this dialogue will help you cope with some of the struggles in your own life. Maybe my humble musings will ease your journey and help you face midlife with grace and dignity. After all, what is life about if not helping each other over the rough spots? (I mean in addition to being seen at trendy clubs in the company of impossibly attractive and talented people.)

And in case some gentle arm-twisting is necessary to convince you that this endeavor will be fun, I offer the following documented testimonies, neither of which was coerced. (Unless, of course, you consider it coercion to ply a person with sugarless gum and hair products — with an overt implication that "there's more where that came from.")

"Lee is a genuinely witty person." — Denise, my sister's friend, who laughed a lot at my jokes *even on the phone* before we met, and who convulsed, albeit gently — she's quite refined, you know — with laughter when we finally did meet *in person*, and who has lived in Geneva, Switzerland, and therefore knows many things.

"Lee has a most charming sense of humor." — Martin, a psychologist at a prestigious university, who, once engaged in conversation, reveals himself to have not even the slightest clue about matters psychological, and whose own personal life is littered with broken marriages, ill-mannered children and poorly groomed housepets, but who, nonetheless, has published several books and is *very* distinguished-looking.

I believe the credibility of these witnesses is beyond reproach. You may now turn the page and begin reading.

1

ONE LUMP OR TWO

Here I sit. A thirty-eight-year-old white female non-smoker with few identified risk factors, perched precariously on the edge of the surgeon's examination table. I have a definite lump in my throat and, unfortunately, several more in my breasts. The giant paper towel I'm swathed in is soaked through under my arms — kind of like Bounty, the quicker-picker-upper — and what I have come to recognize as the acrid smell of my own fear fills my nostrils. I picture this smell radiating from my body in much the way those shimmery waves of heat rise off of July asphalt and wonder for a moment if anyone else in the room notices. I silently reproach the clever copywriter who pronounced my deodorant strong enough for a man. Maybe so, I think, but not strong enough for my fear. Not strong enough to hold its own against my thoughts of death and disfigurement.

In what seems a brilliant flash of insight, I decide this whole ordeal will be easier to endure if I do something radical, like breathe. I realize that I have been holding my breath while awaiting the verdict from the man who is at this very minute professionally fondling my breasts. (And he appears to be fondling at great length, a source of considerable concern to me as there is not that much territory to cover.) So, this is what I've been reduced to, I can't help thinking. This is the true definition of getting old, having to *pay* a man to feel my breasts. I'm looking at this guy and I'm thinking, "This is so weird. You and I graduated from high school the same year. How is it that *you* — who could have sat behind me in homeroom, for crying out loud! — now have the authority to determine my fate?"

His hand returns to the same area several times. My heart races. I study his face closely, trying desperately to read his thoughts. Then, inexplicably, a small cleft in the wall of terror gripping me opens just enough for this one, stunningly inappropriate thought to slip through. "You know," I think, my eyes still fixed intently on his face, "you're kinda cute. I might even have gone to the prom with you. But, make no mistake, buddy, back in 1974 you would have paid *me* to let you do this!"

There is the deep sting of the needle in my flesh, followed by a reassuring gush of fluid. That's a good sign, I think to myself. More stinging, more fluid, more feeling and probing around. And then the fondler speaks. I stop breathing again. Literally holding my future in his hands, he says those three little words that mean so much to a woman, "Nothing worrisome here." In the rush of relief, my lips and tongue go limp. The words "Thank you, God" and "Are you sure?" tumble out of my mouth at once. It comes out more like "Sure, thank you. Are you God?" We both laugh. A natural mistake, he assures me with a wink. We laugh again, and my heart swells with affection and gratitude for my homeroom surgeon, my fondler extraordinaire, my Dr. God.

And that was the first time I was informed that I have "active breasts," a diagnosis my husband is not altogether comfortable with. Dr. God and I assured him that the "activity" took place on a cellular level, but my husband, who is on the road a lot, is not totally appeased. "I'm in a hotel room in Baton Rouge with the Gideon Bible," he says to me, "and you're God-knows-where in Atlanta with active breasts. I believe I have some cause for concern."

As for me, well, I was totally surprised at this diagnosis. I hadn't yet sorted out the philosophical conundrum about how something could exist where nothing was — i.e., how I could have cysts in my breasts when I, in fact, had no breasts. Surely, some natural law has been violated here. But, "active breasts," geez, who knew? They always seemed so passive to me. About the only thing I've seen them do in recent years is quietly inch downward. Apparently, sagging, no matter how gentle, is considered an active process in medical circles. And my husband's fears aside, exactly where am *I* when my breasts are getting all this action? Do they sneak off to a secret life while I'm asleep? Can I expect to suffer breast black-outs, long periods of time when I can't account for their whereabouts? Will they make a Movie of the Week about me — *Sybil Revisited: A Tale of Two Breasts*?

Dr. God was all soothing smiles and reassuring hand pats as he addressed each of my concerns. He just about had me convinced that I might not have charged him full price in 1974 when his appeal abruptly plummeted. Trying to calm my fears, he explained that active breasts were a "normal abnormality . . ." (I'm okay with this so far) ". . . especially among women *of your age*." (Excuse me? I glared at him.) "I mean, hormonal changes occur as women move closer to *menopause*." (What? Now he knew he was in deep and tried to recover.) "I mean, not that you, that is to say, I mean, I *know* you're not menopausal . . . yet."

"Hell, yes, you know that," I thought. "You also know where most of my private moles are. We've been intimate, mister. And this is the way you talk to me, as a 'woman of my age?' I can't believe I ever considered going to the prom with you!"

"Of course, if I had to pick which you were closer to, ha, ha," he had the stupid gall to continue, "puberty or menopause, ha, ha . . ."

Ha, ha indeed! My active breasts and my feeble mind get the picture: we're aging and none too gracefully. Needless to say, my affection for Dr. God pretty much ended on the spot. But not before he had a chance to tell me that it was crucial for us to keep on top of — so to speak — my situation because having so many cysts can make it harder to spot a problem, but that, on the other hand, I was "*really* easy to examine!" Well, as one of my adult literacy students told me when I officiously pointed out that long vowels say their names, "I already *knowed* that!" After all, I'm the one who voluntarily acknowledged there wasn't much territory to cover in the first place. (Which makes me wonder . . . what took him so long, and just how professional was his extensive fondling? Hmm, now that I think about it, I believe he was humming "We May Never Pass This Way Again" — only the official national prom theme of 1974 — during the entire so-called "exam.") He told me to schedule a follow-up appointment, and I told him to write it down because I might not remember by the time I got to the front desk. You know how forgetful premenopausal women are.

A few days later, I went to visit an acquaintance who is a radiologist in the breast care center of a local hospital. Studying my many test results (I can now claim to have appeared topless in several films), she assured me that she saw nothing serious to worry about. "Show me a woman our age who hasn't had some type of breast tissue change," she said. (What is it with this age thing again? And from another woman, no less.) Her diagnosis of my condition made Dr. God's seem downright dignified. "I like to think of them as busy breasts," she said. Busy? Yes, that's my breasts, all right, busy. You know, it's always go, go, go, do, do, do with them. No wonder I'm so tired all the time. We were sitting in her office in "street clothes" — no paper towels — and she casually reached over to use my breast to illustrate a point.

"Do you mind?" she asked.

"Oh, help yourself," I said. "But I have to be honest. You're not my first."

"You tramp," she said and a funny look came across her face as she reached inside my shirt.

"That's doesn't feel like regular breast tissue to you, does it?" I asked.

"No, it doesn't," she said cautiously.

"That's because you have a big handful of Maidenform fiberfill. You won't make contact with my actual skin until you burrow down several more inches."

"Oh," she laughed and looked inside my shirt to help her navigate past the ample padding encasing my busy, but diminutive, breast. "Well," she said when she hit her target, "you can call them active, you can call them busy, but one thing you'll never have to call them again is . . ."

"Perky!" we said in unison, giggling like the teenagers that, despite the cruel betrayal of our flesh, we still believed ourselves to be.

2

LONDON BRIDGE ISN'T THE ONLY THING FALLING AROUND HERE

Of course it's not as if "loss of perkiness" is limited to my busy breasts. Just name a body part, and I will not only be glad to show it to you, I'll even show you where it used to be, which in every case I can think of is several inches to the north. Shortly after my busy breast incident, an ultrasound revealed that I also have "a number" of ovarian cysts. I never had ovarian cysts in my life, so where did they come from? I'll tell you where, they fell from my breasts down to my ovaries, the latest victims of gravity's relentless ravaging of a woman's body. There is a well-worn trail from the top of my body to the bottom left by most of my fleshy parts as they have migrated south. My breasts are headed toward my stomach, my stomach has spilled onto my thighs, my thighs are closing in on my knees, and at this rate I figure my knees should hit land by nightfall on Wednesday of next week. (As it is, they are grazing the tops of my stylish ankle boots.)

Unless the body circumcision — you know, the procedure where all loose skin is pulled tight over your head and neatly snipped off? — is perfected in my lifetime, I have only one alternative. (I know what you're thinking, but I already tried having myself shrink-wrapped. Trust me, it is a tedious process with questionable results.)

So I am left with the hard, ugly truth: exercise. I apologize for using that kind of language, but this issue is important enough for me to resort to shock tactics to get your attention. You don't know me, so you will have to trust me when I tell you that I am staunchly opposed to physical exertion except as it relates to lifting heavy, merchandise-laden shopping bags. (The only other exception I make involves naked bodies, but even then I prefer to be lying prone most of the time, flattering angle and forty-watt lighting *de rigueur*.) I fully expect to be canonized as the patron saint of the indolent immediately upon my death. So it is with a great sense of defeat that I concede on this point, setting my treadmill on high and silently thanking God for the flesh-stabilizing effect of spandex.

Considering my historically deep resistance, it is a source of great consternation among my family and friends that I have embraced this exercise concept so fully, having joined a gym and rarely missing a day since. It's really no mystery. Rule One: Get, like, a really cute trainer. Someone with a name like Sven or Antonio or Marcus. Myself, I picked Dayne because 1) he clearly met all of the appropriate criteria and 2) I knew I'd drive my girlfriends crazy by referring to him as "the Great Dayne." Trust me, finding your own personal Great Dayne will motivate you to the same degree that the thong-clad Bambis in all those aerobics classes past demoralized you. Sustaining a rich fantasy relationship with your trainer is, in fact, key to achieving optimum fitness in record time. Helpful Hint: To facilitate this fantasy, you may have to temporarily suspend your pesky insistence on subject-verb agreement, a practice many trainers apparently hold in low regard.

So I spent my days huffing and puffing and telling myself per my instructions above that "it don't matter" how old I am, I'm going to look great. And then it happened. I was naked, about to get into the shower when I had a head-on collision with reality. Standing in front of a full-length mirror, I was at first excited to see that the eagerly awaited day was upon me — my formerly codependent thighs had gained a measurable degree of autonomy. They no longer touched; there was a clearly defined gap between the tops of them. What a thrill to imagine myself walking in corduroy pants without setting off sparks. My excitement was short-lived, however. Despite the newly created space between my thighs, I was unable to see through to the wall behind me. Something strange and rather squishy-looking was definitely suspended between my legs, obscuring my view. "What in the world . . ." I said aloud. Had my uterus fallen out without my knowing it, I wondered. Part of my intestines? An errant appendix, perhaps? What was this unusual yet vaguely familiar growth? Oh my gosh, I thought, suddenly remembering where I had seen this thing before. It was part of my own anatomy all right; it was my butt! Last I knew it was situated considerably higher. "Gross, gross unfairness!" I screamed. I struggle and sweat to create modest thigh cleavage only to have it reveal severe butt saggage. Where is the justice in this? Well, I consoled myself, compared to what I now know to be the sorry condition of my behind, my upper arms don't seem so bad off after all.

My "unsightly upper arms," as they have come to be known in my intimate circle of friends, have a tale of their own. As I mentioned earlier, I teach in an adult literacy program. I hated to give up my unsightly upper arms because they came in kind of handy in class as I could write on the board and erase in one motion, provided I got enough momentum going. But during a break from teaching I decided to set about paring them down. When I returned to work, I was anxious to share my new achievement with one of my students who was a body builder. When you work with adult literacy students you always look for ways to shore up their shaky self-esteem, pointing out areas where they have succeeded. Freddie, my thirty-two-year-old body-building student, presented a challenge in this area. Whereas the rest of my students were diligent and sincere, Freddie was lazy and full of false bravado. His swaggering demeanor could deplete a reservoir of teacherly compassion in ten seconds flat. Still, I knew he was sensitive about his low reading level, and I always made an extra effort — sometimes through gritted teeth — to highlight skills that he did possess. (Except for his ability to emit unpleasant odors without effort.)

Bubbling with enthusiasm, I rushed to tell Freddie that he had inspired me to start working out with weights. "You are going to be so proud of me, Freddie," I said. "My trainer works with me every day, and I'm really sticking with it." Freddie took a step back, looked me up and down, drew in a deep breath and blew out these exact words, "I hope he give you something for them upper arms."

(Dramatic pause followed by the loud sound of my sucking in air.) "Something for them upper arms? Really? Well, it can't have been easy for you to tell me that, Freddie, but I do so appreciate your brutal honesty. If I seem somewhat flustered, it's only because I didn't realize that the rules governing our conversation had changed. I had no idea that truth was the new order of the day. In that case, let me just return the favor, Freddie, by pointing out, for your own personal edification that *you can't read*, and I don't have time to even begin to list the atrocities you have committed against the English language just in the short exchange we've had here this evening. And just as a helpful aside, Freddie, teeth are not supposed to grow out of the middle of the hard palate, which is where most of yours seem to be coming from, and, finally, just to satisfy my own morbid curiosity, Freddie, what is that odor?"

(All of this was said in my head, of course, as my assertiveness, although much improved, is not what self-help books say it ought to be. Here's a quick insight into this aspect of my personality: If someone shot me, I would still apologize for bleeding on his rug, but I would no longer feel compelled to pay for the cleaning bill.)

I stomped down the hall, arm flesh a-flapping, to seek consolation from my boss, a caring and understanding woman. "I have been found physically wanting by an illiterate man with randomly growing teeth," I cried.

"There, there," she soothed sympathetically, in between loud whoops of laughter. "You just aren't his type, that's all. Your name isn't long enough. A man like that wants a woman with a lot of first names, like Donnna Jo Rae Beth Louise. Makes him think he's gotten his money's worth." She offered me comfort in the form of stale cheese curls and flat Mountain Dew — literacy programs are pathetically underfunded — to make me feel better.

But I didn't feel better, I just felt old. Old and matronly, like the time I was at a conference a few months postpartum and my period launched a surprise attack, leaving me in desperate need of feminine protection. I polled every women in attendance and no one had so much as a Kleenex. Finally, a slim, twenty-year-old waitress, whose pelvis quivered at the mere thought of expanding to accommodate a growing fetus, handed me an ultraslim junior tampon. What was I supposed to do with that? A Q-Tip would have stemmed the tide more effectively. My roommate at the conference, a genteel Southern lady, took one look at "junior" and said, "Oh, honey, you're way beyond that. It's like my mama told me after my first baby was born, 'Ain't nothing fits the same once you done blowed a hole in the thing!'"

3

MID-LIFE SEXUALITY (NOT YOUR AVERAGE OXYMORON)

Well, you knew sooner or later we'd have to talk about the big it — Sex. And I figure there's no better time than right after we've done blowed a hole in the thing! If you are like most of the women in my age bracket, you are now raising Flintstone kids in what is quickly beginning to feel like your Geritol years, and sex is the last thing on your mind. Let me tell you right up front: I am not among those ranks, I have no sympathy for you people whatsoever, sex is the only thing on my mind, and I am having it — a lot! This is my sweet revenge for having had my child at a most unpopular time in history, the '80s.

From anyone's political point of view, the '80s were definitely not about children, at least not for people my age. Small farm animals were more welcome in public places than children were in the 1980s. With my young child in tow, I endured the disdain of many a haughty wait staff in any number of casual dining establishments around the country. Places that nowadays are awash in kiddie cocktails and are cluttered with enough colorful helium balloons to lift the whole damn building a good two feet off the ground if the wind is right.

As one of the four pregnant American women under thirty in 1981, I assure you the family-friendly climate was much chillier then. The seemingly opposing forces of feminism and materialism (among whose ranks I counted myself, depending on who best served my purposes — I'm pretty weak as an idealogue) combined in a curious alliance to wreak havoc on my out-of-sync-with-the-times motherhood. I had the "misfortune" of working at a large university at the time, where I was all but physically accosted by hordes of enlightened women who were aghast at my daring to bring such a wretched symbol of oppression — a belly swollen with child — into the marketplace of ideas. One woman leaned into my ear in a crowded elevator one day and said sotto voce, "You know, there is a cure for that now." I was so startled I thought maybe she had mistaken me for a fellow espionage agent, so I mumbled something about the yellow dog howling at midnight and hustled off at the next floor. When I fully realized the intent of her message, I yelled down the elevator shaft after her, "Yeah, too bad there's no cure for you!" I should have added a snappy "So's your mother!" And they say raging hormones dull your thought processes.

On the other front, I was weary from trying to keep my head above the waters of unbridled greed and materialism which flooded our national impulses — including most of my twenty-something friends — during the go-go decade. All of my (childless) friends were out going, buying and doing. They were worried about closing the big deal, and I was worried about whether or not I'd ever be able to close my jeans again. Shortly after my daughter was born, I didn't know whether to laugh, cry, or scream when one well-meaning(?) power acquaintance gave me a time management book to help me "accomplish more in my day." Hmm, I thought, you mean in addition to my own personal hygiene — a lofty and unattainable goal on many of my early postpartum days. Do I dare to dream so big? Looking at her then, I wondered if we would ever have anything in common again. I sincerely hoped not.

The truth is I, too, was confused about my change in status. I was excited, scared, and overwhelmed all at the same time. This had not been my plan. My fast track to the top did not include a stopover at motherhood at age twenty-four. What's to become of me, I sometimes thought, pressing my hand to my stomach to catch a gentle prenatal flutter. Women aren't even allowed to have cramps in corporate America, much less labor pains. And children? No way.

I had become pregnant so unexpectedly — less than a year after I'd gotten married — that I had had very little time to absorb the major life changes that would occur. It seemed to me that one minute Donna Summer and I were out trying to rustle up some hot stuff, and the very next I was home manufacturing my own milk. It was confusing, but one thing became increasingly clear. Cradling my one-day-old baby in my arms, I knew that immediately returning full-time to the workplace was, for better or worse, no longer an option. Any such thoughts had vaporized in the delivery room the moment I looked into my sweet baby girl's face, her little cherry mouth shaped into a perfect "O" just like Cindy-Lou Who (who was no more than two).

Never have I fallen so fast and so hard. I was completely smitten. Of course, she wasn't playing fair, this eight-pound, five-ounce enchantress. She was simply the most beautiful, most beguiling creature ever fashioned. She was more than fearfully and wonderfully made; she was, with full credit to the Creator, divine. Cheekies so chubby and feeties so fatty that I feared total strangers would be unable to resist eating her up when they passed by on the street. As it was, I had to constantly restrain myself from trying to swallow her whole. Fortunately, the memory of the effort involved in expelling her was still fresh enough to thwart this desire. I was beginning to see that I might have to push my deadline for becoming disgustingly rich and famous back by maybe a week or two.

As much as I reveled in being a mother, even an out-of-step, unprepared one, I still can work up a pretty good lather when I remember how the prevalent thinking of the day cast a shadow over my joy by making me feel I had committed an act of treason against all womankind. I still resent that I wasted precious time worrying how I would recover my "real life" and conform to someone else's idea of or timetable for success. Especially when the same cultural experts who espoused personal fulfillment at any cost are now extolling the virtues of balance and sacrifice and the importance of relationships. Like, no kidding. This is real cutting-edge thinking here. I believe I read somewhere that the world is round, too.

It is mildly amusing to me that the same women who couldn't remember my child's sex ten years ago now, having "discovered" motherhood, send Christmas letters that would embarrass, nay, nauseate, June Cleaver. Last year I trudged through an agonizing end-of-the-year tome from one such woman who devoted a good two pages to regaling me with her five-year-old son's most recent accomplishment — he was hand-picked to pass out the popsicles to his kindergarten class! (One can only guess at the rigorous selection process involved here.) I'm sure the parents will be shelling out big bucks for popsicle training camp next summer to help their young prodigy stay on top of the game. (Sample seminars – "Making the Color/Flavor Connection: Yellow Doesn't Always Mean Banana"; "Beyond the Pencil Holder: More Fun with Popsicle Sticks"; and "Bomb Pops: They're Not Just for Breakfast Anymore.")

This woman's other son has not yet so distinguished himself, but attends a properly prestigious preschool where, the proud mother assured me, "he enjoys the considerable esteem of his peers." Suddenly it's in vogue to lead a life brimming with family values. It's as if children have become the Rolexes of the '90s.

I guess by now we all know that the first thing you have to do if you are a woman with children is realize that no matter what you do someone will think you are wrong. When my daughter was young and I stayed at home with her (at a significant economic sacrifice), people told me that I was throwing all my potential away. This was bad, but, they pointed out helpfully, it didn't alarm them nearly as much as the fact that I wasn't dressing as well as before. (Quelle horreur!) When my daughter was older and I went back to work full-time, people told me I was selfish and shallow . . . and just possibly, according to one concerned woman from my church, setting myself up for a rendezvous with the eternal fires of hell and damnation. Is it really such a daring notion to trust women to make their own decisions? A friend of mine read about a woman who had her tubes tied and untied two times trying to ride the childbirth popularity curve. Tied and untied two times. That is four major operations. Why didn't she just use velcro!

But what does this ranting diatribe have to do with sex, you ask? Well, having a baby in diapers in the dark ages of the early '80s translates into having an adolescent who leaves the house a lot in the mid-'90s. And while many of my friends are now tied down with extremely cute, but time-consuming, little ones — and not dressing nearly as well! — I am relatively footloose and fancy-free. My husband and I are having so much fun. I get to be the girl again. Not the mom, not the wife, but the girl. About two weekends a month anyway. Our daughter's absence has had a dramatic impact on our sex life. As my husband says, "Lee cannot have sex if our daughter is within a one-mile radius, because . . . she might hear something."

Contributing to this rekindled passion is the fact that last year we had my husband neutered. There are some advantages to being older, including knowing positively that you do not want any more children and being able to take steps to permanently guard against that possibility. I can now ovulate with impunity. I thumb my nose at my fertile period. I learned the hard way to distrust other so-called "effective" forms of birth control. (To be fair, what I actually learned the hard way was that screaming "Oh, God" *en flagrante* does not necessarily constitute religious use of one's birth control device. I never made that mistake again!)

I brought my husband home from the doctor's office following his procedure and promptly put him on ice as directed. He fell asleep and an hour later woke up calling my name frantically. "Look at this! They went too far," he wailed. I rushed into the room, afraid of what I was about to see. I looked and laughed. Viewing the "scene of the crime" through the lingering fog of the anesthesia, my husband had mistaken the anatomy-altering effect of ice for that of an overly ambitious surgeon. "Where did it go?" he moaned. "Where is it?"

"Trust me," I told him. "It's in there."

What a fun recuperative period that was. The doctor advised us that it would take about sixteen, um, "times" to flush out all of the remaining sperm. (Now there's a lovely image.) As I had developed a paralyzing fear of pregnancy by this point, and as my husband was going to be traveling a good deal during the next month, the situation seemed pretty clear to me. "Honey," I told him, "sounds like a do-it-yourself job to me." The poor guy. I would call him for progress reports during his travels and ask, "Well? How many can I cross off today? What, that's all? C'mon, man, you gotta do better than that!"

He would tell me that it just wasn't the same without me. Sweet sentiment, but he didn't know I had made plans for us for Valentine's Day. Plans that included my moaning "take me now, my big, strong gelding" from a romantically lit, swanky hotel suite. We didn't have much time to spare. I decided to throw my dignity to the wind and offer him encouragement in another, more tangible form.

"Okay," I said with a shudder, "I'll send you some magazines."

"Really?" he said, barely concealing his excitement. "I was afraid to ask."

"Yeah. In fact, you got two new ones in the mail today. Really glossy covers, full of incredible pictures."

"No kidding?" He couldn't believe I would be so agreeable about this. "Good detail?"

"Great detail. These are some hot dishes, if you know what I mean. No matter how hard I try, mine will never look like the ones in the pictures."

"I have to ask," he ventured hopefully, "any specially themed photo spreads?"

"There is an unbelievable spread called . . . 'The Foods of Tuscany.' They show a close up of full, firm, grilled portobello set against the backdrop of the Ponte Vecchio that will make you faint. And one shot of freshly baked focaccia with Brunelleschi's dome in the background will take your breath away. I'm telling you, it's the Stendahl syndrome by proxy. Florence and food, the strongest aphrodisiacs available without prescription. If these pictures don't do it for you, you have no pulse, man. I may have to go take a cold shower myself."

I could hear him sighing softly on the other end as we hung up, seductive thoughts of garlic and rosemary wooing and winning him over. I decided I would write the editors of *Food & Wine* personally and thank them. I wonder if they ever thought about marketing the magazine as a sex aid for the middle-aged, gastronomically dependent audience.

Of course, I neglected to tell my husband he had gotten that *other* magazine in the mail that day, the really hard-core one. The one that really revs his engine. Yes, I'm talking about *AutoWeek*. (I may well be married to the only gearhead in America who can do a really nice Bearnaise.) This particular issue of *AutoWeek* — I'm ashamed to admit I sneaked a peek — contained several explicit close-ups of the C5 Corvette's 5.7 liter, sequential fuel-injected V8 engine as well as a graphic profile of its suspension system — you know, the one with the independent double-wishbone, tranverse-mounted composite leaf springs, monotube shocks, antiroll bar and optional Z51 performance package. And they send this stuff through the U.S. mail. Without so much as a plain brown wrapper. There was no way I would encourage that filthy habit of his. Liberal-minded or not, there is only so far I am willing to go to get what I want!

4

I MAY BREAK, BUT I WILL NOT BLEND

I used to get so mad at my father when I was growing up because he could make an entire year of holidays vanish in the blink of an eye. "So, today's the last day of school," he'd say to me every June. "Well, pretty soon it'll be the Fourth of July, then Labor Day, and before you know it, you're back in school. Thanksgiving and Christmas are come and gone and, that's it, another year is finished." I thought he was crazy. Anyone with any sense at all knew that summer vacation lasted forever and Christmas never came soon enough.

Then sometime in my late twenties, I noticed that holidays were occurring at closer intervals. It was subtle at first, a minor Halloween/Thanksgiving decoration overlap (same basic colors, so I wasn't overly concerned). When I had to take the pine boughs off the mantle to make room for the Easter eggs, I blamed the federal government. "Darn those Monday holidays, they've thrown off my entire schedule!" This year I actually sent my goddaughter a package in February to simultaneously mark her past September's birthday, Christmas and Valentine's Day. "Happy Birthmastine's Day!" I exclaimed cheerily, vainly attempting to cover my horror at having misplaced nearly six months of my life somewhere.

But that's how aging works. It doesn't have the guts to walk up and look you in the face; it sneaks up in small, insidious ways. Aging insinuates its way into your life with empty promises. "Think how much time and trouble you can save by celebrating three occasions at once," it coos, appealing to your time-starved sensibilities. Holidays that once had distinct, unique identities are lumped together in one nondescript, but ever-so-efficient, "Birthmastine's Day." You don't realize until it's too late that the relatively benign blending of holidays is only a short step away from the most pernicious blending of all, the blending of your very self. Blending just like Nancy Casey, a.k.a., the gray lady.

Nancy Casey was an accountant — which pretty much says it all, I think — at a public relations agency where I once worked. Her main function in life was to issue purchase orders while wearing gray. She wore gray so long and so hard that first her hair and then her skin turned gray — of course, her personality had a jump start on all of this, being without color since the foundation of the world — and then she just simply *was* gray. It was awful because the walls and carpeting of our offices were — you guessed it, gray — and no one could ever tell if Nancy was in her office or not because she blended right in. You just had to stand there, talking into this large expanse of gray nothingness, waiting for a voice to respond, "Do you have backup for all of these purchases?" Nancy Casey blended.

Blending is one of my greatest fears, surpassing even my long-standing fears of the metric system and Silly Putty.

(When I was young my sister told me Silly Putty could come out of its shell unprovoked and attach itself to my body in hideous ways, which accounts for the fact that I have slept with one eye open ever since. Maintaining a putty-free lifestyle is small comfort to me, as I am sure that if Silly Putty is capable of coming out of its shell on its own, then taking a crosstown bus and reading house numbers are not major impediments to its finding me.) Centimeters, plastic eggs, and blending — these are the things that go bump in my night.

Lately, however, the blending question has become more than an academic concern. I have reason to believe that the process may have started. I might as well come clean: I failed to engage people at a recent dinner party. People counted on me, and I let them down. I was dull. I was drab. I was bored out of my mind. And I didn't even try to hide it. Yes, these were tiresome people, people who would have to study for a personality test, but that is all the more reason why I was needed. I should have rallied and feigned interest. I am, after all, a world-class feigner. I am a professional, for crying out loud. I can convince people they are having fun while undergoing, or at least while performing, root canal surgery. After completing three arduous back-to-back root canals on me, my endodontist, weak with laughter, told me it was the most fun she'd ever had in rubber gloves. (Which meant a lot to me, considering she is a dentist and not a proctologist.)

Even the time I broke off the crown on my tooth, mid-sentence, I continued, undeterred, to enthrall a packed banquet hall with an enormously entertaining speech. I mean, I owned those people. I took them up, I took them down, I catapulted them to the very edge of hysteria and effortlessly reined them back in. A broken bicuspid? Ha! I laughed in the face of it. I was brilliant, I was dynamic, I was unflappable, I was . . . well, to be honest, I was in West Virginia at the time, and even with only seven natural teeth in my mouth, I figured I was way ahead of the game. I was something of a local curiosity, in fact. People would look at my mouth — I have a large smile — and marvel, "Dang, you got a lot of teeth! Is all them yours?" Well, I paid for them, didn't I?

In the past twenty years, I can think of only one time when I was less charming than I was at this party. But even then as soon as the last stitch of the episiotomy was pulled tight, I regained my sparkling sense of humor. The obstetrician commented that I was "most pleasant" . . . when I wasn't screaming to have his head served on a platter, that is. Actually, I believe I was demanding to have his head served on a (insert a very bad word here) platter, but you get the idea.

But all of that is in the past. Let's face it, now I'm blending. Just like Nancy Casey. "You are exaggerating. You are not blending!" my husband insists. Oh, really? Then what does account for my lackluster performance at that party? The barometric pressure? Something I ate? Hey, wait one gray, blended minute. I did have a near toxic level of aspartame in my bloodstream that night, which could conceivably cause aberrant behavior. Work with me; it's possible. You remember the Twinkie defense? Why not the Twinkie Light defense, a strategy for the '90s?

After many sleepless nights (and fruitless inquiries into the aspartame industry), I decided there was nothing to do but confront the blending issue directly. I called a woman who was at the party and asked her straight out if she had noticed anything strange about my behavior that night. "At the party?" she asked distantly. "Gosh, were you there? That's funny, I don't remember seeing you."

Was I there? Doesn't remember seeing me? Was this definitive proof of blending or what? It was too horrible. I had to lie down in a darkened room and remain very still for several hours after I hung up the phone. And it was a good thing I did, too, because it turns out I'm going to need all my strength. I just realized that Birthmastine's Day is right around the corner, and I haven't even started my shopping yet!

5

FOR SALE BY OWNER: SLIGHTLY USED SKYLIGHT, TWO-BY-FOURS OPTIONAL

The desperation of aging makes you do crazy things. Like asking your older sister for advice. I was going to ask my older sister Sam if she thought I should color my hair. Then I remembered she was the same sister who convinced me to "do something" about my caterpillar-like eyebrows when I was in tenth grade. As the anointed beauty guru of our family — she had been to New York City on at least two separate occasions — her ruling was immutable. "Something must be done," she said decisively, "and I'm the one to do it." I nodded in agreement, unwittingly giving her permission to commit what can only be classified as a hate crime against my face.

Dismissing the tweezers as inadequate for the mammoth task before her, she snatched up a razor with a brand-new blade and began shaving my unruly eyebrows into submission. Yes, I said, shaving. A moment of silence, please. The result was not exactly the graceful arch I had pictured. The words "burn victim" don't begin to describe it. Browless, I went to school. Browless, I went to church. Browless, I lived, and browless, I was certain, I would die — of acute embarrassment. When my other sister Eileen saw me, she bowed her head and said three Hail Mary's for the repose of my soul, certain that death by public humiliation was very near. It was a tenth-grade nightmare beyond all imagination. Not even Bill Clinton could have felt my pain.

Still, watching the gray hairs on my thirty-nine-year-old head multiply faster than rabbits was enough to make me consider giving Sam another chance. Shoot, I reasoned, in the years since the Great Shave-Off Sam had actually lived in New York City for extended periods of time. Besides, it had been at least a year since I'd had my last revenge dream about her. (The one where she's held down by a large German woman named Hilda and given a bikini wax without sedation.) I had nothing to lose but my gray, I decided. As I reached for the phone, it rang. When I picked it up, I heard Sam's voice at the other end. It was fate, confirming my renewed faith in my sister.

"You must come over at once!" she blurted. The desperation was unmistakable.

"What's wrong?" I asked in a panic.

"It's fallen off." She choked out the words between deep sobs.

"What? What has fallen?" I asked urgently.

"The house . . . the light . . . completely fallen off," she mumbled nearly unintelligibly.

Sam had just moved into a newly built house, and I had visions of roofs collapsing and walls sinking into the ground. "Tell me what has fallen," I instructed her, using the same measured tone that those "Rescue 911" operators employ when delivering babies over the phone.

"Just fallen, fallen completely off." It was futile to try to get an answer out of her when she was like this. I left for her house immediately.

I braced myself for the devastation I would witness when I arrived at the house, but as I pulled up the driveway, everything looked in tact. Must be an interior wall, I thought. The door was open so I went in, calling to my sister as I wandered from room to undevastated room. Everything looked fine, but Sam was nowhere to be found. Finally, I heard some whimpering coming from upstairs and followed it, expecting to find one of the cats mewing in protest at its new surroundings. Instead, the trail of sighs led me to Sam's bedroom, where I found her slumped down in the corner, her faced buried in her hands.

"What is going on?" I asked in confusion.

"I didn't really think it would happen to me. But it's fallen," she said.

"What has fallen?" I demanded impatiently.

"This!" she said, lifting her head. "My face. It has fallen totally off."

"Oh, is that all?" I asked, relieved. "I thought it was your roof trusses or your floor joists."

She was unmoved by my knowledge of construction terms.

"It's my own fault," she continued. "What is a woman my age doing building a house with all these windows? 'I want a house that's flooded with natural light,' I said. 'I want a skylight over my vanity,' I said. What was I thinking? This," she said, pointing to her face, "is what a skylight over your vanity gets you — a fallen face."

"Your face hasn't fallen," I said.

"You're just humoring me," she said. "Look me in the eye and say that," she challenged.

I cupped her chins in my hand, looked into her eyes and said solemnly, "Your face has not fallen."

"No?" she ventured cautiously.

"No," I said. I paused for a moment before adding, "Okay, it has maybe 'slidden.' But just a little." This was as close as I might ever get to eyebrow payback, and I was going to make the most of it.

"Don't toy with me," she pleaded. "This is not 'slidden' face," she said, pinching a fold of flesh from under her chin. "This is fallen face."

"That," I said, "is not face at all. That is another anatomical structure entirely."

"What is it?"

"You don't want to know," I told her.

"Yes, I do. I have to know. You have to tell me," she said, near tears.

"Okay, but it's not pretty," I said, feeling a bit flushed with the power I suddenly held over her. I could almost feel my eyebrows growing thick. "That is wattle."

"Wattle?" she asked, confused.

"Yes, wattle," I replied. "A fleshy, wrinkled fold of skin hanging from the neck or throat, characteristic of chickens, turkeys, some lizards, and, in your case, certain women over forty."

"I'm going to vomit now," she said calmly, closing her eyes.

"Although, to be precise, you do not actually have wattle," I continued authoritatively. "I don't?" she asked hopefully.

"No, you have what is termed 'incipient wattle.' Of course, incipient wattle inevitably progresses to full-blown wattle," I explained.

"How much time do I have?" she asked.

"Well, don't be shocked if next Thanksgiving you feel an uncontrollable urge to crawl onto the serving platter and surround yourself with cranberries. If you catch my drift."

She cringed. This was fun.

"In other words, incipient wattle today, pin feathers tomorrow. I'll be gobbling by the end of next week," she said with grim resignation.

I couldn't stand it any longer. I burst out laughing. "Oh, get a grip," I said. Your face has not fallen, and you do not have wattle, incipient or otherwise."

"Really?" she asked.

"Really," I told her. "But you are right about one thing. There is entirely too much light in this bedroom. My hair looks like Nancy Casey's in this light. In fact, I wanted to ask you — "

"As in Nancy Casey, the gray lady?" Sam gasped, horrified. "Well, that does it," she added definitively. "I'm selling this house. How many women's lives must be destroyed before I take action?"

"Isn't that kind of extreme?" I asked. "Let's call Eileen and see what she thinks. She lives in Florida, a state known for bright sunlight. She must have developed some coping skills."

"True," Sam agreed. "Plus she's even older than we are."

We called our older sister who assured us via speaker phone that, based on her years of experience with unforgiving sunlight, selling Sam's house was unnecessary. "Which is not to say that it doesn't need some alterations," she explained. "First, hang fully lined hotel/motel type window coverings on every pane of glass in the house. Next, put low-wattage bulbs in all light fixtures and drape gauze over all lamps. And most important," Eileen added emphatically, "board up every last skylight. Climb out on the roof with a load of two-by-fours yourself if you have to, but cover them. Believe me, it's the only way."

She was beyond brilliant.

"You do realize that the actual appearance of your face

will not change, but your perception of it will. At our age, that's worth a lot," she concluded.

"And this will work for my hair as well?" I asked.

"What's wrong with your hair?" Eileen asked.

"It's really looking gray, especially in this light. I thought maybe I should do something with it."

Sam seemed to perk up at the sound of these words. "Do something with it," she repeated.

"Yeah, highlight or color it. What do you think?"

"Hmm," said Eileen as she mulled over this possibility.

Suddenly, I caught Sam's reflection in the mirror. She was more animated than she had been all day. She looked positively energized. What is going on, I wondered.

"No, you don't want to highlight it or color it," said Sam, walking toward me with her hand behind her back. Was that a gleam in her eye?

Instinctively, I started backing away. "I don't?" I asked.

"No," she said, moving closer to me. "Why bother with all that mess when it's so much simpler to . . . shave it off!" She whipped a razor out from behind her back and thrust it high in the air above my head. "It'll be such a good look for you. You don't have to shave all of it, just the gray parts." She was poised to strike when I shrieked, "No! Not this time, you New York City dropout, you beauty guru imposter. I'm out of here."

"What's going on there?" Eileen screamed.

"She's got a razor, Eileen, and she's not afraid to use it," I said breathlessly.

"Run, Lee, run," shouted Eileen.

"That's what I'm doing," I called as I made a beeline for the door. Charging down the hall, the razor-wielding Sam in hot pursuit, I could hear the disembodied voice of Eileen on the abandoned speaker phone back in the bedroom.

"Hail Mary, full of grace," she intoned, "the Lord is with thee . . ."

If you ever think fate is calling you on the phone, hang up!

6

HAVEN'T GOT TIME FOR THE PAIN (WELL, MAYBE JUST A FEW MINUTES)

As if the fact of being thirty-nine years old isn't painful enough, now I am also expected to interact in meaningful ways with people who think Pulp Fiction was John Travolta's debut effort. Who think Tony Bennett and Mel Torme got their start on MTV. I am talking about people whose brains contain less memory than a low-end fax machine. Let me share with you this incident that in and of itself is completely odious and vile, but seemed exceptionally unfair considering that it came less than twenty-four hours after my thirty-ninth birthday — an occasion I celebrated by going to the driver's license renewal center where the clerk suggested it might be time to start calculating my age in dog years. People are so funny.

In the very throes of this postbirthday devastation, the proportions of which exceeded seismic measurements I entered an innocent-looking music store. I was casually wandering around, mentally debating which posed a greater threat to the future of civilization — nuclear holocaust or a

Porno for Pyros concert — when I accidentally came upon a CD of an old Carly Simon album, circa 1978. It was just sitting there in a bin — right out in the open, ready to assail the heart and mind of any unsuspecting, emotionally compromised woman in my demographic group. There was no tamper-resistant safety packaging, no conspicuous label reading: "Warning — Listening to this music will induce memories so painfully bittersweet that putting an ice pick through your brain will seem a pleasurable alternative."

As furious as I was at this callous disregard for public safety, I was, as the moth to the flame, drawn. I had a fleeting moment of sanity wherein I tried to reason with myself: "Just walk away now," I told myself, "and no one gets hurt." But as any common junkie can tell you, reason is no match for the monkey and its sick, twisted desires. And of course the denial. "I can handle this music. It won't make me feel old. I'm not trying to relive the past. I can stop any time. It doesn't affect me." (As for that unfortunate incident last summer — the time I drove off the road, blinded by tears, because they unexpectedly played "Help Me" by Joni Mitchell during an "All '70s Weekend" — well, that was strictly coincidence.)

With a mixture of fear and awe, I gingerly picked up the CD, according it all the respect due a holy icon of its stature. A flood of memories was unleashed just by reading the song titles. Songs I hadn't even thought of in years, but which now exploded into my consciousness, explicit images of high-spirited, mortgage-free youth hanging on every literate lyric. (I have to ask, can you really picture anyone, twenty years from now, having this reaction to the following lyrics from a Blind Melon song: "So, I wrecked your life, what the heck"?) I took a deep breath and steadied myself against the wall. Steadied myself against the torrent of years that came rushing by me at breakneck speed. I held my ground. Youth is not everything, I repeated like a mantra. I made a mental list of all of the blessings in my life now: A husband who loves me, a daughter I adore and a dog who walks backward and barks at my purse. Plus good skin and nice nails. My life was full. So what if nearly twenty years had gone by? I was not that old, I concluded.

I strode to the front and plunked down my purchase on the checkout counter, confident that I was prepared for whatever digitally remastered memories were encoded on this disc. And then it happened. This, this, child — no make that embryo — behind the counter cavalierly picked up the soundtrack to my life, tossed it in the air a couple times, and said, "So, like, what kind of music is this?" Trying not to panic — after all, I thought, it was an old, somewhat obscure, album — I replied, "Oh, it's old, but it's Carly Simon." I thought that would say it all. But, no, he persisted. This embryo with a name tag said, "So, like, who's Carly Simon?" Hyperventilating, I summoned up the strength to offer this informative reply: "She's, like, Carly Simon. She sings. Songs. And stuff." Clueless, the embryo just stared at me. "Oh, I know," I said, certain this would turn the key, "she used to be married to James Taylor." I hated defining her identity in such limited terms, but I was desperate to see a spark of recognition in the embryo's glazed eyes. He remained silent, and I, with sinking heart, realized the awful truth: He had no earthly idea who James Taylor was.

And that's the last thing I remember before I lost consciousness. When at last I came to, Zack (or Dylan or whatever his tragically hip name was) politely asked if there was anything he could do for me. I asked him if he would be kind enough to help me gather up the loose love beads that had broken and scattered when I fell off my platform shoes.

As I hobbled out of the store, a broken woman, I wondered if Zack/Dylan could picture himself someday in the distant future, frustrated at his inability to communicate to the younger generation how deeply the Meat Puppets had touched his life.

7

BURNED BY THE FLAME OF YOUTH

Of all of the rituals women employ to stave off the debilitating effects of aging, surely the total facial makeover remains one of the most time-honored and humiliating. My friend Kate read that world-renowned makeup artist Anthony Roberts was coming to Atlanta and for a mere fifty dollars would be only too happy to laugh in your face and say things like, "Oh, my dear, someone apparently ignored your instructions not to be resuscitated." Kate was steamed about her husband's spending so much money on golf and wanted to frivolously waste some herself to even the score.

"Hmm, let me get this straight," I said. "You're mad at your husband, so it's going to cost me fifty dollars?"

"Exactly. Now get ready because our appointments are for ten this morning."

"Are you crazy? I can't be ready by ten. It'll take me two hours just to do my makeup and hair," I said. "Plus I have to find something stylish to wear."

"It's a makeover. Who cares what you look like going in?"

Kate said. "They can't take our 'before' pictures without our permission. Lurlene said so."

"Who the heck is Lurlene?" I asked.

"She's the young cosmetics woman at Macy's, and she's ever so earnest," Kate replied. "Her exact words to me, as she gazed sincerely into my eyes were, 'Oh, no, ma'am, I don't believe they'd dare do that with you.' What exactly do you think she meant by that? Well, in any case, Lurlene would not lie."

"I'm glad you and Lurlene have bonded so beautifully," I said, "but you just don't get it, do you?"

"Get what?"

"You're not going to wear any makeup to a makeover?"

"Well, no, I'm not."

"Have you lost your mind? That's like saying you aren't going to clean your house before the cleaning lady comes. You wouldn't dream of doing that, would you?" I asked.

"Well, of course not," Kate answered impatiently. "Do you think I want her to know what a slob I really am?"

"Then why would you expose your naked face to public ridicule and scorn? Listen to me, you greenhorn. Makeovers are no place for amateurs. Lurlene's ostensible earnestness aside, Mr. Anthony Roberts has one goal in mind: to indict us on charges of criminal ugliness, no matter how good we look in our 'before' pictures, so that we can buy our freedom with his beauty products. If you go in there naked-faced, you will be convicted before you can say 'alphahydroxy.' By the time he's through sentencing you, there won't be an eye pencil left unsharpened in the state of Georgia. Your Visa card, not to mention your ego, will never recover."

"Oh, you're right. I don't know what I was thinking," she said. "It's just that Lurlene seemed so innocent, so believable — hey — you don't think Lurlene was in on it, do you?" Kate asked.

"I'm not saying that," I replied. "Certainly, I've seen that scam before, but she could just as easily be a pawn in their dirty little game. It's possible she's in over her head."

"Oh, that poor girl," Kate sighed. "The makeover business is nasty."

"Indeed it is," I said knowingly, and we set about putting our best face forward.

The truth is I didn't have all that much experience with pricey in-salon makeovers myself — enduring in-kitchen Mary Kay makeovers had been more my unfortunate experience — but I had a pretty good idea of how they worked. I knew these people preyed shamelessly on a woman's insecurities for profit. I imagined it would go something like this: A woman tentatively approaches the appointment desk, eyes downcast, "Do you think Mr. Roberts would see me next week? I know it's a lot to ask, what with my T-zone having such irregular borders and all — it's a temporary hormonal problem I'm having — but I'm willing to pay extra." Her request is discreetly handled by a nonthreatening Lurlene-type who makes her feel safe and convinces her to let down her guard. Once the poor woman actually says the words, "Oh, this is going to be fun," they know they've got her! The unsuspecting woman then shows up, naively naked-faced, at the appointed hour, expecting to be warmly greeted by her confidante Lurlene — who, by the way, graciously assured the woman earlier that her irregular T-zone, while obviously problematic, would be handled with the utmost professionalism. To her great shock, she is promptly handed over to a cadre of severely made-up women, dressed from head to toe in faux Left Bank black. By the time she is led into the inner sanctum to see the great and powerful

Oz, she is too intimidated to ask why she needs three different toners and four different replenishers when she only has one face. (Just as she could never admit to her hair stylist that she has trimmed her own bangs between cuts. "The ends just started breaking off," she'll say. "It was really weird.") No, her only thought at this point is getting her credit limit upped so that she can begin to make amends for every untightened pore on her unclarified face.

Well, Kate and I would not be led as sheep to the slaughter. We were going in prepared!

"Mr. Roberts will see you now," said the surprisingly — and, I thought, deceptively — friendly handmaiden. As steeled as I was for this experience, the words still struck terror in my heart. Kate and I were ushered in separately — of course, divide and conquer — but I was determined not to crumble. I was presented to Mr. Roberts, an imposing, patrician-looking man with a silver mane. He said nothing as he surveyed me up and down, clipboard in hand. I coughed nervously. I can't let him get to me, I thought. His eyes darted in staccato movements from my hair to my nails to my probably ill-chosen hosiery. After a few moments of silence, he spoke. "And this is your look?" he asked.

"Yes, this is it. Pretty much. Mr. Roberts, sir," I answered, feeling my chest tighten.

A hint of derision quivered at the corners of his mouth. "Yes, of course, it would be," he sniffed and began marking up the form on his clipboard, finishing each notation with a great flourish.

More nerve-wracking silence followed as he scribbled away on his clipboard. Why didn't I wear the black dress, I scolded myself. It's so much more sophisticated. And lip liner, I can't believe I forgot lip liner. Oh great, I thought, any minute now a fashion police S.W.A.T. team is going to rush the place and take me down. My rap sheet will identify me as Lee "Demode" Potts. Just as I was about to ask for my one phone call, Mr. Roberts began firing questions at me. "What is your blood type? Do you have a history of fainting? Are you allergic to anesthesia?" Routine beauty questions.

He paused dramatically after I finished answering, then turned, looked at me eye to eye and asked purposefully, "Would you wear red lipstick?"

"Yes?" I replied somewhat unsure of what the correct answer was.

"Tell me again," he demanded. "Would you really wear it?"

"Yes, I would," I said more strongly. "I would definitely wear it."

"But, you must convince me that you would not simply wear it, but *wear* it, inhabit it, color your life with it, or I shall not waste my time prescribing it for you."

"Oh, but I would wear it," I pleaded, the need for red lipstick suddenly becoming even more urgent than the need for my own personal salt lick on days twenty-one through twenty-seven of my cycle. "Indeed, I would do more than wear it, or inhabit it, I would become it. My heart, my soul, my very essence would be red lipstick, now and for all eternity. Please, please, you must prescribe it for me. I will prove myself worthy."

"Very well, then. I'm going to take a chance on you," he answered and dispatched one of the handmaidens to the vault to fetch a thirty-dollar tube of Flame Eternale, my soul's new essence in an emollient-rich base. I felt so blessed.

The actual reconstruction of my face passed in a blur. I was giddy with delight after Mr. Roberts pronounced my skin, eyes and lips to be "definitely not awful." Imagine, he said that! About me, a commoner! Of course, he had to take points off for my having eyebrows that looked like "two unfinished sentences," but that was only fair. (I thought it wise to keep mum about the Shave-Off.)

The makeover turned into a virtual lovefest, with the handmaidens fawning over me, Mr. Roberts hovering nearby to ensure the proper foundation coverage, and everyone showering compliments on me. (Although Mr. Roberts's compliments were a bit tricky to decipher, couched as they were in pompous affectation.) Didn't I tire of people telling me how beautiful I was, the handmaidens wanted to know. (Actually, I have nearly unlimited stamina in that area.) Didn't I drive my husband absolutely wild with my incredible eyes, they asked repeatedly. (No, but he has been known to get pretty worked up over my stuffed peppers.) Oh, how could I have been so wrong about these people? They were committed to my welfare, to helping me unleash the beauty that lay dormant inside of me, the beauty that Flame Eternale would now set ablaze forevermore.

When at last I was allowed to rejoin Kate, we both stood and stared at each other's transformation. I spoke first. "I am Flame Eternale," I said.

"And I," she said momentously, "I am Tulipe Mystique."

The intensity of the moment gave both of us goose bumps. We couldn't buy our forty-seven different "prescriptions" fast enough, although I skipped all the skin-care items and doubled up on the glamour products, preferring style over substance any day.

"Who would have thought happiness like this could be had for a mere three hundred dollars, plus tax?" I marveled.

"And to think you said they would try to take advantage of us," Kate said. "Intimidate us into buying lots of useless cosmetics. Everyone was so nice."

"I know. I never felt any pressure from anyone. I mean, I practically had to beg Mr. Roberts to let me get the Flame Eternale. I was really wrong about this."

"You sure were," Kate laughed. "But, then again, they could tell they weren't dealing with a couple of Pikers, either."

"Yeah, that's for sure." I added in agreement.

And so we two savvy women of the '90s went on our merry way, proving once again that shameless flattery outsells sneering degradation every time.

8

IN SICKNESS AND IN HEALTH (BUT NEVER IN THE SAME CAR)

Convalescence. Now there's a word that just reeks of aging. Although I was not the convalesce-ee, the one doing the actual convalescing, I am here to tell you that being the convalesce-or, the one facilitating the convalescing, is no day at the beach. Especially when the convalesce-ee is a person of the male persuasion whom I at an earlier point in time — for reasons totally inconceivable to me during the period of his confinement and my indentured servitude — considered a suitable marriage partner.

I recently saw a story on the local news about the horrors of a new form of thrill-seeking sweeping bars across the country — bear wrestling. It's true. Bored bar patrons are doing this for sport. You may wonder who volunteers to wrestle a bear for fun. I'll tell you who, wives who have just spent endless weeks attending to convalescing husbands, that's who. Bear wrestling or possibly a tour of Bosnia seem positively recreational after what these woman have been through.

The weeks leading up to and following my husband's neck surgery cannot be recounted in detail here as they would depict human suffering — mine — entirely too graphic for this medium. Women, of course, are genetically engineered to withstand more pain than men, as women's biology dictates that they will, at some point in their lives, face the most excruciatingly painful experience imaginable — going one-on-one with an aggressive panty liner adhesive strip. Tears spring to my eyes just thinking about it.

Women also know that suffering through unintentional depilation in the name of feminine hygiene (or random incidents of near death and dismemberment for that matter) is nothing compared to a man's annual bout with the common cold. My own personal husband has uttered these words — with a straight face — after his first cough of the cold and flu season for the past fifteen years, "I hope, (cough, cough) it's nothing . . . serious." The first few years of marriage, I expressed concern, then reassurance, then mild amusement at this ritual. Now I just feel flat out homicidal whenever I hear a man — any man — so much as clearing his throat during the winter months. (One little bald man nearly suffered a heart attack right there at the Duke of Suds car wash because I bellowed, "Give it up, cue ball, I'm not falling for it!" in response to what I perceived to be his too persistent "ahem-ing" at me. Turns out he was trying to discreetly point out that my skirt was tucked into my panty hose. An honest mistake, okay?)

But having surgery to repair a ruptured cervical disc is admittedly a bit more serious than a cold. I was immensely relieved and grateful when the surgery was successfully completed, and I brought my husband home the next day to nurse him back to health. As a testimony to my husband's recuperative powers, in no time at all his behavior enabled me to jettison all thoughts of sympathy in favor of fantasies about "making it look like an accident."

"Why," my husband asked every three to five minutes, "do I feel so terrible?" About the fortieth time he said that, I sat down in front of him and helped him evaluate the situation logically. "Let's see," I said, "less than forty-eight hours ago, you had enough needles stuck in you to turn you into a human pin cushion, had your head bolted into something resembling a medieval torture device, had your neck sliced open, exposing the very nerve center of your body to God and man alike, had the five disc fragments pressing on your spinal nerves yanked out, were stitched back together and dispatched to your room where you refused pain medication. Why do you feel so lousy, Bill? Gee, I have no idea. I'm completely stumped."

He was also mystified as to why he was still unable, three whole days postoperative, to swing a golf club. Had the surgery failed? And why, he wondered further, had the doctor's orders included the sinister admonition to "rest completely" if the surgery had really done the job? "You're right, Bill," I finally conceded. "The doctor is clearly buying time. He doesn't want you to realize that he completely screwed up the surgery, so he told you not to move much for a few weeks, allowing him the time to transfer all his assets to a Swiss bank account and leave the country without a trace. After all, any neurosurgeon worth his salt would have placed a seven iron in your hands even before you regained consciousness."

I then pointed out to my husband that if even I — a known hypochondriac and expecter of the worst — thought his fears were premature, then he was probably overreacting. This conversation ensued:

ME: How come when I am in the throes of a health crisis, you tell me not to worry about it?

HIM: Because everything you almost have is fatal.

What's the point of worrying about it when you'll be gone soon anyway?

ME: So all those times you were telling me I'd be fine, you were really making plans for what you'd do with my side of the closet?

HIM: No. Here's my point. If you're dying, there's no point investing time in worrying about your condition. But, if you're going to be around for a while — like me — then quality of life becomes a legitimate concern.

ME: Hey, Bill, just remember this: Nobody likes a malingerer. People will respect me for my ability to die quickly. They'll resent you for hanging on indefinitely.

It was then that I began mentally working out the logistics of sneaking up on him and dropping a heavy object directly behind his right ear, causing him to react with enough force to snap his head completely off, thus ending this whole ugly episode. Then I remembered all of the sweet, thoughtful things he had done over the years, and I softened. Plus sneaking up behind him would have involved my uncomfortably wedging myself in the roughly two inches of space between the wall and the back of the recliner where, TV remote in hand, he had taken root.

But, by far, the most punishing aspect of his rehabilitation for both of us was his inability to drive. I had to drive him everywhere for an entire month. Imagine my surprise to learn that after twenty-one years of driving, I knew absolutely nothing about the correct way to maneuver a car through traffic. I am grateful beyond printable words for my husband's many helpful tips which have enriched my life in ways too numerous to count. However, married women in my neighborhood now speak my name in reverent tones, knowing that the only thing standing between them and a chauffeur's cap is a slim half inch of unherniated cervical disc.

Bear in mind that I was not driving around just any husband, I was driving the man who holds the unofficial title of "Mr. Car." (It's unofficial because not everyone understands the importance of, for example, trunk etiquette; not everyone admits to the urgency of the question, "Is there ever any justification for putting the atlas on the right-hand side of the trunk instead of the left?" I'm afraid my husband takes a pretty hard line on this issue. "What is more threatening to our well-being as a nation," he argues, "than trunk chaos, which is surely where we are headed if exceptions to the rule are allowed. Where will it end, jumper cables left twisted and tangled, extraneous items tossed in the trunk at random and allowed to rot?" I often think of the trunk as a large gum wrapper repository, but I keep these heretical thoughts pretty much to myself.)

I spent a month chauffeuring Mr. Car and having my turn-signaling, lane-changing, and braking judgments called into question. I thought I displayed extreme grace and restraint overall. There was one time when I had to pull over and say, "Look, buddy, let's understand each other. I own you right now. You go when I say and how I say, or you don't go. I could dump you on the side of the road, spray-paint 'Trunk Etiquette Hardliner' on your forehead, and you would be mincemeat in a matter of seconds. You're in the heart of enemy territory." (We were in the parking lot of a discount store frequented by harried mothers of small, whining children — notorious and unapologetic practitioners of trunk sloppiness. Carbon dating has been used to determine the age of the Happy Meal remains in the cars of many of these women.)

Still, we coexisted without serious personal injury until "The Big One." This was my breaking point. I was carefully backing out of a parking space at Publix when he suddenly started barking orders at me. "Get in the right lane now!" he commanded. My immediate reflex was to do exactly as he instructed, but then I realized that there was no "right" or "wrong" lane, no "right" or "left" lane for that matter. All the parking spaces pointed in the same direction; there was only one lane, "the" lane, and I was backing into it very nicely. Postsurgical irritability or not, he had pushed too far. I decided to call his bluff. "There is only one lane, dear, the lane I am in," I told him, my voice rising. "So I assume that it would be the right lane." Exposed, he backpedaled quickly, saying he meant for me to make sure I got in the right lane to exit the parking lot "or we might not . . ." his voice trailed off. Since there were at least three ways to exit from this parking lot, and since each exit lane was at least fifty yards away from us, I was unable to share his sense of urgency about our lane situation. "Or we might not what?" I demanded to know. "What would happen? We might not ever make it out of the Publix parking lot? We would just drive around and around forever in grocery store–parking lot limbo? What is the terrible, irreversible, life-altering thing that would happen to us should I fail to get into the 'right' lane even before shifting out of reverse from the parking stall? Answer me that!"

Of course, he had no reasonable answer except that he felt a God-given obligation to criticize my every move behind the wheel on general principle. He was, after all, Mr. Car. Not in all circles, I reminded him not so gently. After we got home, he confessed that he was not really worried back there in the parking lot. He said he knew that even with me driving we would eventually have found our way out. "We could have found our way out of Katmandu, for that matter."

"Why," I asked, "because I would have asked for directions?"

"No," he replied, "because we have all the information we could ever need almost at our very fingertips, securely held in the appointed atlas section on the *left*-hand side of the trunk."

I rolled my eyes.

"We have the ability and resources to control our own destiny," he continued with the zeal of a pompadored preacher. "That's the power of a well-organized trunk — personal freedom." He paused reflectively then. "If I could just get people to realize that. They need to know," he murmured, his head now in his hands, "but I'm only one person." His aching desire to break the stranglehold of trunk ignorance was palpable.

My hardened heart melted. His compassion for the uninformed masses, his commitment to improving the lot of all humanity despite his own pain and Demerol-induced haze was both touching and ennobling. I realized I was in the presence of a true visionary, a man dedicated to empowering lives through proper trunk etiquette. Let others continue to drive in circles without exit agendas. I'll not have time for such frivolity, I thought. I'll proudly serve as chauffeur on the front lines as long as I'm needed, grateful for my small part in advancing the cause. "No longer will you be a lone voice in the wilderness," I told my husband. "From this day forward I'll be by your side, fighting the good fight, until every broken umbrella, fossilized Teddy Graham and mutant lint ball has been exorcised from every trunk in America!"

His eyes misted up as he embraced me, his new convert, into the fold. "This has always been a dream of mine," he said. Exhausted, he collapsed into the recliner — actually dropping the remote control in the process — and dozed off. I covered him with a blanket and grabbed the remote. "I salute you, Mr. Car," I whispered into his ear. "You'll always be the official title holder of my heart." Who could have guessed a few days earlier that his convalescence would forge this new and profound closeness between us? Now if he would just sleep long enough to let me watch "NYPD Blue" in peace, I might even give up bear wrestling.

9

YOUR PARADIGM OR MINE?

I think adulthood can best be described as the stage of life that begins the first time you spend your own money on items you can neither wear nor eat, such as snow tires. Snow tires are not fun, but they are not the worst part about adulthood. The worst part is that people expect you to act like a grown-up, especially at work. Look, I will accept personal responsibility and be accountable for my actions and even pay taxes, but I remain morally opposed to most of what else passes for grown-up behavior in our society, such as pretension, self-importance, and just general stuffiness. I find most business situations particularly intolerable, as most of the time they involve patently boring stuff pedaled by patently boring grown-ups.

As a public relations consultant, I feel like such a fraud, appearing to listen intently as clients explain the importance of their products and services to me. Everything from "treatment protocols appropriate for any degree of osteoporotic involvement" to "geosynthetic applications for polypropylene extruded fiber." I nod convincingly and produce the requisite "aha's," but inside my eyes have glazed completely over. I have mastered the art of appearing outwardly interested, while inwardly screaming, "Who cares?"

After sitting through one especially grueling, minutia-packed presentation on the latest advances in cardboard containerization (can you stand the drama of it?), I wanted to grab the guy by the lapels and demand, "Is all this detail really necessary? How critical an issue is this? It's not like we're talking about eye shadow here, okay?" Isn't there an OSHA rule that says for every hour you spend engaged in boring grown-up work, you get an hour off to devote to really important matters? You know, like compiling a list of "Things I'd Like To Do To Jimmy Smits (Melted Chocolate Optional)."

Compounding my problem with being a grown-up is the fact that I hate speaking the language. I hate lingo. I hate buzz words. Grown-up business people love this stuff. They talk about everything vis-à-vis something else and make frequent paradigm shifts. One client fixated on the word "synergy" and insisted I use it in every single piece of literature we produced for his company. I am now so synergistic I am greater than the sum of myself.

Moreover, in order to pass in the adult world I have had to say things like "We are trying to identify the variables that may be contributing to your uncharacteristic confusion surrounding this issue" when I yearned to speak the plain, unadorned truth of my youth: "You are so totally not getting this, you idiot!" I've been forced to respond to highly questionable data with a low-key "Is that so?" in a roomful of puffed-up marketing specialists (the kind that have haircuts in lieu of personalities) when a straightforward "Na-uh, you so lie!" would have been much more to the point. Sometimes, I ache to throw in an old-fashioned, "You are not the boss of me," just for the heck of it.

Before you get all superior on me, I want you to know I

scored a very respectable 760 on the verbal section of the GRE. (All I'll tell you about my math score is that I did, in fact, get one. I don't mind addition, but subtraction strikes me as being so negative.) The only vocabulary word I didn't know was "sinecure," which means a cushy job with little real responsibility. Ironic, the very thing I've been looking for my entire life, and I didn't know it when it was staring me in the face.

The other thing that really bugs me about communicating as a grown-up is that is you have to take turns talking. I hate that. I view any time I have to spend listening to someone else talk as cutting directly into the time I get to talk. I like it much better when I am with my friends and we all talk at the same time, and no one ever finishes a sentence, or at least not the same one they started, and everyone goes home not having a clue as to what went on, but knowing somehow that we had a great time. To be perfectly honest, I like it the absolute best when I am the only one talking and everyone else sits enraptured. I was recently in a commercial that was a dream assignment for me. The director wanted to go for a very spontaneous, natural feel. As a warm-up, he directed me to look into the camera and "just start talking" about the product. Realizing he had no clue to whom he was giving direction — his naiveté was touching — I explicitly asked him, "Exactly how long do you want me to talk?" His casual response? "Oh, as long as you have something to say." I could tell he didn't understand my point. "Let me put this another way," I said. "How much film did you bring?" He laughed and called "Action." (He was so totally not getting it.) I did as he directed.

By the time I finished talking — several minutes later — a hushed silence had fallen on the set. People were staring at me with their mouths open and hair blown back. The director seemed to be in some sort of trance. He hated it, I thought. Finally, he spoke. "That was . . . good . . . great . . . really great . . . amazing, actually. Now, if we could just get you to open up a bit."

We worked together again (at his request, no less), and the entire spot was precisely scripted except for my parts, which simply read, "Lee talks here." What can I say to that except obviously his understanding vis-à-vis my performance shifted paradigmatically. In other words, "He finally so totally got it!" (Synergistically speaking, that is.)

10

WARNING: READING IS HAZARDOUS TO YOUR HEALTH

"You get too many magazines," I told my husband, as I hoisted a stack of periodicals that represented the depletion of one-tenth of all the forestland in America. "I think your magazines get magazines."

"I just have a lot of interests," he said. "If you had more interests, you'd get more magazines too."

"By interests, I presume you mean hobbies. I have plenty of hobbies, but they don't publish magazines for my hobbies," I answered.

"There is a specialty publication for every market segment imaginable," my husband said. "There have to be magazines for your hobbies."

"Really? Like what?" I asked. "*Hypochondria Monthly*? *Recreational Depression*?"

"What about *Impending Doom Digest*," he suggested.

"Ah, yes," I said. "Motto: 'Fewer laughs than an Ingmar Bergman film fest.'"

"You could be the editor," he said.

"Reading about your hobbies is a sign of old age, Bill.

Much better to be actively engaged in them like me." I said.

The truth is, being buried under an avalanche of glossy paper is a small price to pay to ensure that my husband leaves this world with his body parts in roughly the same configuration as they were when he came into it. A casual glance at the titles of the magazines my husband gets tells you that the man's interests can be divided into two categories: activities related to food and activities with a survival rate of less than 10 percent. The only thing that keeps him home whipping egg whites into a frenzy instead of jumping out of a plane, hanging off a mountain or racing cars at speeds recorded in triple digits is my incredibly effective begging. That, and threats to dump a load of used Kleenex in his trunk if he kills himself in one of these insane pursuits.

Don't even ask how fast he used to drive the Corvette he had before I met him. He told me that if the car went over 110 mph, the radio came on spontaneously. When I asked him his top speed, he simply said that he had enjoyed the convenience of hands-free radio on more than one occasion. I shuddered. I can't know stuff like this. I am the queen of caution. The kind of person who wears sunscreen at night. Who thinks water beds should come with flotation devices, just in case. "Physical caution, emotional risk," those are my words to live by.

My husband may have no known physical fear, but let me tell you what makes him really nervous. Television cameras, or more specifically the thought of having to speak in front of one. I hosted four different talk shows in two different cities for several years, and I can count on one finger — okay, three fingers — the number of tapings he attended. It's not that he didn't support me; he was just petrified to be that close to a live camera. (Which is only the biggest rush on earth.) It didn't matter that I was the one actually on; he was a wreck.

He couldn't even watch the shows after they were taped because it made him so nervous. "What if you can't think of what to say next?" he'd fret, wringing his hands. I would point out that first of all, the show was complete, so we already knew that I didn't screw up. And second of all, not having something to say has never exactly been a problem for me.

If reading about car racing keeps my husband from actually doing it, then I figure the same principle applies to one of my favorite hobbies, hypochondria. That is, maybe thinking I have every disease known to man will keep me from actually getting any of them. (Mental illness at its finest.) So, every now and then, I diagnose myself with some affliction, an affliction which my personal team of physicians and other health-care professionals fail to confirm. But I say, why trust the opinion of people who rely on training and experience, who deal in scientific data and verifiable findings, over the opinion of someone like me who employs *the* state-of-the art diagnostic tool — *People* magazine? Talk about your gold standard. No matter what ailment I secretly believe I have contracted, rest assured a famous person will talk about it in *People*, listing all of my symptoms with astonishing accuracy. (See, I do know the value of a good publication.)

Of course, it's not my symptoms that my doctor ever takes issue with; it's my diagnoses. "You never make things up, Lee," said Dr. Allen, putting a Sesame Street Band-Aid over the spot on my arm where a nurse had just drawn blood. "You just consistently leap to drastically wrong conclusions." "It's a gift," I said modestly. He adjusted the Band-Aid so that Big Bird's face wasn't scrunched, a gesture that, in my mind, planted him squarely in the camp of those who consider the practice of medicine an art. "I appreciate your indignation at your body shifting gears on you," he said, "but I assure you all the changes you've described are quite normal."

"That may be," I replied, "but I can't help feeling like the little boy who, when informed that first grade, unlike kindergarten, lasted all day, put his hands on his hips and said, 'Well, who the heck signed me up for this?'"

He laughed. "Nobody signed us up, but we are all getting older." Before I could stick him with a needle, he slyly added, "But, you don't show it like I do. You look fabulous. Medically speaking, of course." Nice save.

"So, let me get this straight. I'm okay?" I asked.

"You're okay," he answered.

"You really heard everything I told you?"

"I did."

"You're not being dismissive? Because you know I hate that."

"I'm not, and I do," he replied.

"You know you have to answer all my questions because if you don't — " I started.

" — you will make up the answers," he finished.

"Right. And the answers I make up — "

" — will be much worse than the truth," he replied dutifully.

"Very good," I said. I was impressed with the progress he'd made since I first became his patient. He was definitely trainable.

"Lee," he said, "you are quite delightful."

"Thank you," I said.

"And," he continued, "stark raving mad."

"I work at it."

I got up to leave, feeling fairly confident that I would not expire on the drive home. But he just couldn't leave well enough alone. No, he had to call after me, "Maybe I'll see you at The Who concert Wednesday night."

Excuse me? The Who concert? Was he saying he was actually going to see The Who, right in the middle of the week? "Oh, sure, that's right, Doc," I felt like saying, "you have nothing better to do than stay out 'til midnight, groovin' with a bunch of aging rockers on a work night. I mean, why sit around reading those boring old medical journals when you can take a ride on the 'Magic Bus'? Hey, sleep in every morning, for all I care. It's not like you have my case to think about!"

Shoot, he was probably double dating with my gynecologist, another so-called dedicated caregiver. I am forever running into her in the grocery store where she all but admits negligence to me. "Oh, every time you see me here," she says laughing, "I'm a mess from digging in the garden all day." Digging in the garden, huh? Well that's certainly a wise use of her time, wouldn't you say? You never know when a patient might have trouble with her, oh, I don't know, say, rutabagas. These doctors blatantly act as if they have their own lives to live — regularly leaving home without my chart on their persons — and then they wonder why I'm just a little concerned about the level of care I'm getting. Unbelievable.

Well, this one wasn't getting away with it today, I decided. I turned on my heel, walked back into Exam Room 3, pulled out the latest issue of *People* from under my coat and slapped it down on the counter in front of him.

"Okay, Concert-man," I said. "Since you seem to have so much free time on your hands, I'm sure you won't mind taking a few minutes to explain this to me." I pointed to an article detailing a mysterious set of symptoms currently plaguing a mildly talented TV personality.

"Oh, no, not again with the *People* magazine," he pleaded.

"Hey, don't blame me. It was in your waiting room," I answered. "Now quit trying to dodge the issue."

"Lee," he said, "whatever this condition is, I swear you do not have it."

"You won't even look at it, will you?" I asked, holding the magazine under his nose.

"I don't have to," he said. "I've told you, you can't go by these articles. They are so general and vague, they could apply to anyone," he said.

"Aha! Then you admit it!" I said triumphantly.

"Admit what?" he asked, confused.

"That theoretically I could have this condition, whatever it is," I said.

"What are you talking about?" he asked, really confused.

"You said these symptoms could apply to anyone, right?" I said.

"Right." he answered.

"And I am anyone, am I not?" I asked.

He saw where I was going with this. "Yes, but — " he began.

"But, nothing," I said definitively. "I rest my case."

I'll tell you one thing, he won't be so quick to accept free tickets to a midweek concert again. In the end, we struck a deal. He agreed to at least look at the *People* article if I agreed to stay away from all materials even slightly medical in nature, which I assumed meant I couldn't order Dr. Pepper with my Extra Value Meal. At least not without a signed permission slip.

I can be very reasonable. My husband and I have even reached a compromise about his magazines. He can subscribe to any new magazine he wants as long as I get to videotape him reading it aloud.

11

FLING, FLANG, FLUNG

Hey, here's a big news flash for you: Women Have Sexual Fantasies. And the late twentieth century marketplace being what it is, exploiting these fantasies is now big business. Everywhere you turn, there's a headline screaming the latest provocative finding from some study on women's secret desires. Books, magazines and movies are all cashing in on the sudden interest in this previously underexplored terrain. You know, "Women on Top," "Boys on the Side," "A Perfect Graham Cracker Crust on the Bottom." Okay, so I made the last one up, but the stress is getting to me already. Because you just know what's next. Now that women's fantasies are hot copy, it won't be enough for us to be merely sexual, we'll all feel compelled to be SEXUAL. We won't be able to have some half-baked little fantasy anymore, we'll all have to have FANTASIES. The experts will make sure of it.

That's a lot of pressure to put on someone like me who is extremely married. Not that I'm not a SEXUAL woman with really great FANTASIES or anything, but I feel like I'm betraying my husband when I have even the most fleeting thought about anyone else. Where some women draw dotted lines, I draw double yellow ones. On the rare occasions that I dream about another man, even a made-up, nonexistent one, I never get to do anything "good" with him. I never even get to kiss him. In every single one of these dreams, I always end up saying the same thing: "I can't, I'm married." Even when I am deep in REM territory, I am apparently afraid an alarm will sound, alerting my husband and the world at large that I have committed mental adultery, or at the very least, mental heavy petting.

That's not to say, however, that I have remained totally and boringly chaste. In the nearly seventeen years that my husband and I have been married, I have successfully pulled off four or five mental flings by adhering to a carefully prescribed set of conditions. And that's my real beef with all this publicity about women and their fantasies: Amidst all the hype and headlines, no one is bothering to point out the dangers of fantasizing without the necessary precautions. It is completely irresponsible to turn women loose without so much as a hint of the calamity that awaits them if they haven't been trained how to handle a fantasy properly.

Rule Number One: If you are a married woman, you cannot have a fantasy fling until you first make provisions for your husband. That is to say, you must create an acceptable explanation as to why your husband would not object to your involvement before you begin. However, please tell me you are not naive enough to think you are supposed to tell him about your fantasy relationship. I just mean that you must set up conditions under which it would be acceptable for you, a married woman, to be with your fling person.

This step is critical because the biggest danger with a fantasy is that the mere power of suggestion will set in motion some horrible unintended result, such as payback. What started as a harmless bit of private amusement in your head will end with your real flesh-and-blood husband walking in the door and stating unequivocally and for reasons even he can't explain that he is leaving for Costa Rica with a supple-skinned twenty-year-old named Tiffani — yes, with an "i." And while it's true that this tragic turn of events will rip your heart from your body and cause you immeasurable pain and suffering, (including, but not limited to, perpetually sallow skin) no one will even feel sorry for you because, let's face it, you asked for it. Asked for it, nothing; you caused it outright. In your heart, you know it never would have happened if you hadn't spent a good thirty seconds imagining yourself — casually sans husband — as Katharine in *The English Patient* while you were stopped at the red light outside the orthodontist's office last Wednesday. (And there were minors in the car at the time!)

It is, therefore, imperative that you construct an explanation that is as plausible and repercussion-free as possible for your husband. Unacceptable choices: Husband has left you or husband has died. For reasons I have just explained, you cannot even kid about these things. Furthermore, be aware of the more subtle limits implied in that rule. Don't make the mistake of thinking that just because you haven't actually killed your husband off in your fantasy, you are in the clear. I myself once fell into this trap, and it was scary. This is what happened.

One summer when my husband was traveling a lot, I was caught off guard by the intensity of my reaction to Timothy Dalton, and I got sloppy. In my rush to be with Timothy Dalton (not as himself actually, but as Mr. Rochester in the PBS version of *Jane Eyre*), I violated the most basic rule in all flingdom: I failed to provide a satisfactory and safe explanation for my husband's noninvolvement in my mental affair. My sister, gathering all the pertinent preliminary details from me, uncovered my error. "Well, it's obvious that you and Rochester belong together," she said, "but what provisions have you made for Bill?"

"Um," I said impatiently, "I don't know. We'll just say he, like, snapped." (So careless, so shoddy.)

"Snapped?" she repeated.

"Yeah, you know, just one day, up and snapped and is kind of temporarily catatonic and just wants to go off to live by himself for a while. Everybody feels sorry for me because I have been such a good and faithful wife and even he wants me to be with Rochester now because it makes him feel less guilty for snapping and everything."

"I don't know, that's kind of risky. We've never given anyone an actual condition such as snapping before. Aren't you going over the line here?" she asked.

"Look, you wouldn't even know there were rules for these things if I hadn't told you. You've been playing Russian roulette with mental flings for years and now you're trying to act like some big expert. You're just jealous because I married a man who had the decency to snap and leave me with Timothy Dalton," I said haughtily.

"That was uncalled for, but as long as you brought it up, how can you ignore what happened in the Michael Andrews case?" she responded.

Oooh. She scored a direct hit with that one. In her younger and cockier days, my sister had her own over-the-top experience (with Michael Andrews) that had disastrous consequences, all because she broke the second cardinal rule of flinging: A fling can never, ever be with a person, most especially a married person, from your real life. These affairs must remain as far into the realm of fantasy as possible.

My sister had made Michael Andrews, a real person she had known fifteen years and three cities ago, the object of a week-long mental relationship. She, unmarried at the time, used the woefully inadequate and dangerous premise that Michael's wife "just suddenly left him" to explain his availability. She persisted despite my warnings. She was so far gone that at one point she angrily accused me of "not supporting her in the relationship." No kidding I didn't support her; she was playing with fire. I tried to explain that it didn't matter that she had not seen this person for fifteen years and in all likelihood would never see him again in her life. She still couldn't mentally mess with the life of a real — and married — person. But she had had a dream about him and was determined to fling away. "He lives fifteen hundred miles from here. Who will it hurt?" were her exact words.

Well, I guess I don't have to tell you how it ended. Through a series of "accidents," we received news of long-ago, faraway Michael Andrews — without warning, his wife of eighteen years had left him and moved to Las Vegas to live with some guy who worked for Sigfried and Roy. Coincidence? I don't think so. Michael was devastated, and my sister, who had no real romantic interest in him or desire to help him piece his life back together, felt responsible. "I never meant to ruin his life," she sobbed. But it was a little late for that.

So, you can see why the Michael Andrews reference brought me up short. I immediately revised my plans for Rochester and myself according to the prescribed guidelines. But, what if I were too late? What if the damage had already been done? I had no peace (or sleep) for the next several weeks, monitoring my husband round the clock for any signs of snapping. If he stared into space for more than five seconds, I called his name frantically to make sure he was still functional. If he delayed more than an instant in answering me, I shook him, begging him to "come back to me." After about a month of this, he pulled me aside and said he was concerned about my behavior. "What's going on with you?" he asked. "It's like something in you has snapped or something." Do I have to spell it out for you? Break the rules, pay the price.

All of that is not to scare you totally off the idea of flinging, but to impress upon you how crucial a solid beginning premise is. That being said, let me now share with you the conditions under which the fling itself should operate. The absolutely most ideal fling is one that has been directly ordained by God. If you can get God's imprimatur on your fling, you are pretty much home free. This is not as far-fetched as it may sound. For example, say there has been some horrible catastrophic event, leaving your husband unconscious for an indefinite period of time and you and Mel Gibson as the only other survivors. God comes down and, time being of the essence, directly orders you and Mel to begin repopulating the earth. Then, of course, you must make the supreme sacrifice and proceed. A word of caution, though. If God himself does not order the fling, do not proceed, even if it seems to you that the catastrophe criterion has been clearly met. Years ago on "Guiding Light," Ed and Claire assumed their spouses had been killed during a terrible siege on Beirut, and without actually hearing the voice of God, took it upon themselves to begin the repopulation process. Well, guess what? After all the smoke had cleared, not only were the spouses still alive, but they were less than impressed with Ed and Claire's selfless attempt to perpetuate the human race. Nine months later, Claire gave birth to Ed's baby and then eventually went insane (as well as to another network). I'm telling you, it pays to wait for God's clear direction on these things.

Now, granted, the God scenario must be used sparingly. Therefore, the next best setup for a guilt- and consequence-free fling is the modified disaster/circumstances-beyond-your-control situation. In the modified disaster situation, life as we know it is not destroyed, only temporarily disrupted, which means there is no need for God to issue a dictate . . . and also no humanitarian basis for "repopulation," so I recommend you stop well short of that. But at least you and your fling get to be thrown together in intimate circumstances and experience underlying sexual tension. Plus, he comes to appreciate your great inner strength in the face of adversity as well as your ability to look glamorous in the midst of a natural disaster. (Hey, despite some necessary restrictions, this is still supposed to be a fantasy.)

After much research among my women friends, I have determined the following to be the safest and most popular disaster/circumstances-beyond-your-control setups:

The Flood — You and Andy Garcia are separated from the rest of the group by a sudden flood. Raging, ice-cold flood waters rip off most of your clothes (although any figure flaws remain tastefully camouflaged), forcing the two of you to huddle together to keep deadly hypothermia at bay.

The Snowstorm — You are having a perfectly above-board business lunch with Denzel Washington when a freakish (you know, like in July) snowstorm hits, bringing the entire city to a standstill. You manage to make it across the street to his room at the Ritz Carlton where you must spend the night because all the roadways have been closed.

The Blackout — You and your colleague, Pierce Brosnan, are the only ones working late when a power outage plunges the city into inky blackness. Obviously, it is not safe for you to leave the building, so the two of you make microwave popcorn — courtesy of the emergency generator — and wait for daylight together on the conference room couch.

Important Note: In all of these cases, your husband is out

of the country on very important business, so he doesn't worry about you. When he returns, he is so glad you are okay that he overlooks where you spent the night.

Obviously, there are endless variations on these themes, and I encourage you to adapt them to fit your needs. Flinging, done well and within the limits, can provide hours of convenient, free and wholesome fun. But in closing, let me issue one more warning. Never forget that even experienced flingers must follow the rules. I was painfully reminded of that just last year when I foolishly let what should have been a simple, legal fling extend into a "relationship." I got stung pretty bad.

George Clooney had been pursuing me relentlessly through two and a half seasons of "ER." He was perfect fling material, of course, but he wanted more. He led me hook, line and sinker to believe that he wanted — needed actually — a relationship with me. I kept resisting, but every Thursday night, there he was, blinking out Morse-coded messages of love to me with those soulful, bad-boy eyes. "Blink, blink-blink, bliiiink, (I love you, Lee), blink-blink-blink, bliiiink (I want you, Lee)." Sometimes it was so blatant, it was embarrassing. My friends would call me after the show and say, "Please, Lee, give him a chance. He needs you so much." So I did. I realize I should have known better, so please don't sic Dr. Laura on me. But, foolish or not, can you imagine how much it hurt, come Christmas last year, to see him cavorting around with Michelle Pfeiffer up there on the big screen? Oh, like she's just so gorgeous he couldn't help himself, right? Please, how about a little self-control, Mr. Clooney?

The second he knew he had me, he was out having *One Fine Day* with her. I know it sounds petty, but I'm glad the movie was a bomb. Serves them both right. And to think

I broke up with Timothy Dalton, to whom I had been completely faithful for more than four years, for him. I felt so used.

These are the real stories behind the racy fantasy headlines. The stories you won't hear anywhere else. Just remember: fling with caution.

12

THEY'RE BA-ACK

Eighteen years ago a friend and I inadvertently went out on a date with two convicted criminals named Mike and Tony. Oh, grow up, it happens. (Of course, pray to God it never happens to you.) I tell you this now because I have recently learned a painful lesson: The older you get, the greater the chances that a dreadful incident from your past will return to haunt you. Mushroom farmers-cum-drug dealers-cum-entrepreneurs, Mike and Tony defy easy description. In fact, an incomplete description of Tony (or "Tone," as he is affectionately known) is what led to my regrettable decision to be the "fourth" on that fateful night so many years ago.

It was the summer after our senior year in college, and my friend and I were housesitting for her vacationing parents. We were determined to pack in as much adventure as possible before real life, complete with real jobs, began in September. This is a daunting task in a town of about three thousand, but like most know-it-all twenty-one-year-olds, we welcomed the challenge.

We were sound asleep one morning when the phone, blaring like an air-raid siren on steroids, abruptly woke us at the ungodly hour of eleven A.M. (We'd only crawled into bed a few hours earlier.) Ginny answered it, and I heard her mumbling her agreement that last night had been "pretty wild." I was struggling to recall if I was any part of that wildness when I heard her straightforward, but polite rebuff: "Thanks for the offer, but, see, we generally don't get 'wasted' before noon . . . and, well, we don't ever do that, either before or after noon."

My mind was racing. Well, as much as it could on three hours of sleep. Who was this person? My memories of the previous night were somewhat patchy. I remembered that this cute guy I'd had a crush on a few summers before had asked me out and had driven Ginny and me to the party. I remembered dancing very closely with my cute guy somewhere between my second and third rum and Coke. (Which was about two and a half more than I usually had or could handle.) I remembered thinking that you could pass out at this party and never fall down because there were so many people packed in the room. I remembered my shoe falling off at one point and being utterly stymied about how to put it back on. (Perhaps this was between the fifth and sixth rum and Coke?) I remembered thanking my cute guy profusely for so brilliantly cracking the shoe code — he effortlessly slipped it back on my foot as if he'd been doing it all his life — as well as for agreeing not to drink so he could drive me home.

But try as I might, I could not remember meeting anyone who would call and propose untoward activities at eleven o'clock in the morning. Just then Ginny said, "Well, yes, we do eat and swim, but again, not before noon." I was right in her face at this point, demanding to know who it was. She covered the phone with her hand and whispered, "It's Mike. From last night. He's asking if we want to go swimming or out to eat."

"Who?" I asked again, still confused.

"Oh, that's just Lee," Ginny said into the receiver. "She's staying with me. Well, I don't know, I'd have to ask her. What's your cousin's name? What does he look like?"

I began wildly gesticulating my disapproval for the emerging plan.

"Look," said Ginny to Mike. "We'll talk it over and call you back in a little while."

"Who is this Mike person and did we make him any promises we have no intention of keeping?" I asked, vowing never to even drink Coke again, much less Coke with rum in it.

"No, it's just Mike. You know, Mike, from last night," she replied matter-of-factly.

I shook my head "no."

"Remember I came over and told you I smelled someone wearing Polo? Well, I followed the trail, and it ended at Mike."

"You smelled him at a party, so now I have to go out with his cousin?" I asked.

"Lee, it was Polo," she said with finality.

Unfortunately, I completely understood the insane allure of Polo. Several months earlier I had tracked a middle-aged, moderately unattractive gentleman through the entire Kmart shoe department on Christmas Eve just to get a whiff. What was supposed to be a quick stop to load up on AAA batteries turned into a forty-five-minute discount store safari.

"Do I at least get to know his name?" I asked with resignation.

"His name is Tony, and Mike says he's really funny," she said a little too enthusiastically.

We decided on the dinner option because I was not

putting on a bathing suit for someone I didn't know, and Ginny, who had stopped shaving her legs earlier in the summer as a political statement, was determined not to compromise her beliefs — even for Polo. Seven P.M. came, and my heart was pounding. We saw their car pull up in front of Ginny's house. A tasteful dark-blue Saab. So far, so good. (Like axe murderers can't drive Saabs.) I saw Mike get out. He was relatively decent looking. Tall, kind of lanky, dirty blond hair, wearing jeans and a cotton sweater. Okay, some dermabrasion wouldn't have hurt, but he appeared normal enough. And then I saw my mystery date, Tone, as he unfolded himself from the passenger seat. All 250 pounds of him. Remember the fat Elvis stamp that everyone rejected? Remember Nick Tortelli, Carla's ex-husband on "Cheers"? If the two of them had a love child, it would be Tone.

The closer they got to the front door, the louder my whimpering got. Ginny opened the door, and I was face to face with the largest swatch of polyester I'd ever seen in my life. (And I had seen *Saturday Night Fever* six times.) Tone was an absolute vision in Quiana. There was not a natural fiber to be found on him. Unless, of course, you counted body hair, which was a different story altogether.

And what a conversationalist. "Hi, I'm, like, Tony, heh-heh, but everyone calls me, like, Tone and that. I don't know why, heh-heh. It's, like, funny, you know? Heh-heh." Oh, yeah, Tone, it's, like, downright hilarious. Tone and I sat in the backseat of the car, where I plastered myself against the door. I figured falling out on a sharp turn couldn't be any worse than what I was already enduring. And there were a lot of sharp turns on this mountain road leading to the restaurant. I thought Mike was taking them hard on purpose to launch me across the seat into Tone's Quiana-draped arms. In between thinking up painful ways for

Ginny to die, I made a few stabs at conversation.

"So, Tone, what do you do?" I asked.

"I'm, like, into mushrooms and that," he said.

"You mean eating them . . . and that?" I continued.

"No, growing them," he replied, setting me straight. "Hey, that was kind of a joke you made, huh? Heh-heh, you're, like, funny and that," he marvelled.

"And that," I nodded.

It turns out old Tone was a sort of mushroom magnate, having descended from one of the most influential mushroom farm families in the tricounty area. Heck, he was practically royalty, having been crowned king of the Fungus Festival for two years running. Our fascinating conversation was interrupted when Mike took what was clearly a twenty-five-mph turn at seventy-five. Ginny and I both gulped loudly. Mike apologized and said he was still getting used to driving this car.

"Oh, did you just get it?" I asked.

"No, it's Tone's," he said.

"And he makes you drive him around because he's the mushroom king?"

"Not exactly," said Mike. "He's not allowed to drive yet. See, I got out first."

"Of the military?" Ginny asked.

"Of prison, actually," replied Mike, careening around yet another turn in the road.

"Yeah, but we did wear uniforms and that," Tone, the quipster, quickly added.

I am a person who cannot stand awkward silences even when they are preferable to awkward conversation, so I jumped right in with, "Let me guess, the charge was vehicular homicide."

"Reduced to involuntary manslaughter. That vehicular

homicide charge was so bogus," Mike explained, as he slammed on the brakes to avoid rear-ending the car ahead of us.

We finally did find out that Mike and Tone, those wacky guys, were just kidding about the nature of the charges. True, they had been nabbed for a moving violation, but it was the controlled substances the police found in their car that caused the real problem. And in a show of great cousinly solidarity, Tone said he was driving — even though it was really Mike — because with Mike's previous driving record, his license would have been permanently revoked on the spot. Tone took the rap, man. A condition of his parole was that he not operate a moving vehicle for six months.

"So, we never really killed anybody or anything," Tone laughed. I felt so reassured that I decided to let Ginny arrange all my dates for me from then on. After all, I'd never found anyone of Tone's calibre on my own, had I? The rest of the date included the following highlights:

1) A stop at a poorly lit bar that Ginny and I had heard had developed a shady reputation in recent years. Mike and Tone insisted they had never been there before, but when we walked in, the bartender, a sixty-year-old Lithuanian midget standing on a stool, yelled across the room, "Hey, Mr. Mike, Mr. Tony, the usual?" Mike mumbled something about cutting the legs off his stool before we left.

2) Mike's suggestion that we go to an even shadier establishment to see a strip show performed by a fifty-five-year-old woman with a football-shaped surgical scar on her abdomen. It was not easy talking him out of that.

3) My pretending to be unconscious on the way home so Tone would leave me alone. When Tone asked, "What's wrong with her?" Ginny replied, "Oh, she has this condition. She just lapses into a coma sometimes. It has some-

thing to do with her nasal passages." Oddly enough, that seemed to satisfy him.

We made it home alive, and through the creative use of makeup and strategically placed hair pieces, managed to duck Mike and Tone for the rest of the summer. Yet, from time to time in the eighteen years since that incredible night, I have wondered whatever became of the dynamic duo. Well, the wondering is over because three months ago, Mike rose like a phoenix from the ashes to haunt Ginny's life again. He tracked her down through an elaborate system of contacts he'd developed over the years. (Not all of them legal, I'm sure.) Since she was still single, Mike felt certain the two of them were destined to be together. Ginny tried her best to disabuse him of that notion. She flat-out refused to 1) meet him in a public place, 2) go to his apartment, or 3) invite him to hers, but she finally had to concede that she could not prevent him from driving past her building if he wanted to, this being a free country and all. "Okay, it's a start," Mike said, encouraged. (She's applying to the witness protection program even as I write this.)

"So, what on earth have they been doing all this time?" I asked Ginny when she told me about the phone call.

"Well, they found something they liked and stuck with it," she said.

"Prison?" I asked.

"No, mushrooms," she answered. "Well, actually there were some drug and prison interludes, followed by a stint in the city sewer department, but all that ended back in the late '80s. For the past seven years they've been running a successful specialty mushroom business. You know, high-end products like portobellos and shitakes. They sell to places all over the country. They wheel, they deal. I think Tone's even traded in his Quiana for Armani."

"Unbelievable," I said.

"And get this, they call the company 'Fun Guys Do Fungi,'" she snorted.

"That would be, like, a joke and that, heh-heh," I said. "Gee, I guess they're not just your average felons anymore," I added almost wistfully.

Ginny laughed and said, "Lee, I'm telling you, those guys are an enigma with a capital 'N.'"

And so they are. I guess the longer you live, the more you are shocked and amazed at the twists life takes. The older I get, the more I realize how impossible it is to predict the way things will turn out because life is just too full of surprises. Still, I think it would be a really good idea if some kind of legislation were enacted to regulate the dispensing of Polo. That stuff remains too dangerously available to suit me. There are some surprises I — and the world — could do without.

13

MEMORY? WHAT MEMORY?

People say that one of the nicest parts about getting older is having memories to look back on. There's only one catch; the older you get, the less you can remember. This deterioration poses a particular threat to me because I am widely regarded as the official keeper of the memory among my family and friends. For years they have counted on me to keep track of all the incidentals of their lives — little things like what they wore on their first dates, when they got their first kiss and what they named their first-born child.

I've been a walking diary for everyone in my life. Sometimes for amusement my oldest friends will call me up at three in the morning and try to stump me with questions like: "Okay, what was the name of the 'new' girl in our third-grade class, the one who only stayed a few months and who was absent nearly the whole time?"

"Oh please," I laugh, "That's so easy, it's embarrassing. Her name was Charlene Roddy. And Sister Loretta (who I just happen to recall was precisely 112 years old at the time) called her 'Miss Fancy Work' because she missed so much school that all the 'X's' after her name in the roll book looked liked cross stitch." (Which now that I think about it was an unnecessarily cruel and embarrassing thing to announce to the rest of the class, and I feel really crummy for publicizing it now. Please forgive me, Charlene, wherever you are.)

Considering how I have exposed poor Charlene, I suppose it is only fitting that I now find myself engaged in a roll call ritual of my own. Remember how your mother would stand there, look you straight in the face and run through every name in your immediate and extended family until she got to yours? And sometimes she never did come up with a match. Like the time I heard my friend's mother recite the entire litany of family members, including Spanky the dog and Mouse the cat, and finally throw up her hands in complete frustration saying, "Oh, that girl over there with the long legs, the one I gave birth to without the aid of medication, what is that child's name?" Oh, how we all laughed. Guess what? It's not so funny anymore.

I have exactly one husband, one child and one dog, it shouldn't be that difficult to keep them straight. Yet, more and more, I seem to confuse them. I absentmindedly murmured "good doggie" the other night while I was rubbing my husband's neck. (Well, he *is* really hairy — though nothing like Tone!) And as for my increasing tendency to yell "C'mon, Ruckus, let's go" to hurry my pokey fifteen-year-old daughter along, all I can say is there are impressive similarities between a teenager and a dog. Well, think about it. They both love to sleep all day, they both constantly beg for treats and you can't reason with either of them. (Not to mention that our dog has been spayed, a procedure I'm seriously considering for my shapely daughter, in light of the response she evokes in teenaged boys.)

But it's not just people's names I can't recall, it's also the names of everyday objects. I routinely have to run through a laundry list of unrelated items before I hit on the one I mean to say. Like, I'll say, "I think there is something wrong with the dishwasher, car door, lamppost, insecticide, refrigerator. That's it, the refrigerator!"

To complicate matters further, my husband has a funny little idiosyncrasy. Without realizing it, he will often say the exact opposite of what he means. (Yeah, I know, all men do that on a large scale, but he does it with specific words.) For instance, when it is ninety-eight degrees outside, he will come in the house, dripping with sweat, and exclaim that he is freezing. He regularly takes things *up* to the basement and *down* to the attic. Can you even imagine the conversations we are going to have as the years progress? In the middle of a terrible January blizzard, he'll be yelling about how hot it is, and I'll be telling him to turn up the garden hose, bookmark, umbrella stand, thermostat!!

I'm telling you, about the only thing I retain these days is water. (Sadly, some things never change.) And yet, my memories from two and three decades ago remain very strong. It's information from two minutes ago that I can't hold in my mind. For example, I can tell you with absolute certainty that I wore a blue-and-white-striped bra to my eighth-grade graduation, but I can't remember if I even put one on — striped or not — this morning.

And that's the kind of thing that really concerns me, not the forgetting of a random word or two, but the wholesale forgetting of entire incidents. From what my older sisters tell me, the closer you get to menopause, the more you have to fear in this department. My sister Eileen, who is single, relayed to me how she went to bed one night, fully clothed in pajamas and socks, and woke up the next morning stark naked. She assumes she had a hot flash in the night, but has no conscious recollection of either the hot flash or the removal of her clothing. (The one thing she is certain of is that she had no assistance in taking off her clothes, a fact she notes with more than a little disappointment.)

My other sister, Sam, went around for weeks thinking she had suddenly developed psychic powers in midlife because she seemed to know what people were going to do before they did it. I was excited about her new abilities, seeing endless ways to exploit them for our own profit, but I started becoming suspicious of her "gift" when she turned her prediction powers loose on me. She knew things about me, all right, but curiously enough, her knowledge always seemed to coincide with information I had left on her voice mail. I watched our psychic-powered money machine come to a screeching halt as I put two and two together: Estrogen deprivation had apparently erased from her mind any conscious memory of retrieving her messages, but she had retained the essence of the messages themselves. She wasn't psychic, she was menopausal. Boy, were we disappointed.

I have managed to keep my clothes on (well, most of the time), and I haven't started predicting the future yet, but in the past three months I haven't come home from the grocery store one time with everything I was supposed to get. I guess the writing is on the wall, which, according to my husband, Franklin Covey's Man of the Year, is not the place it needs to be. "It's time for you to start writing things down in an organized fashion, like I do," he instructs me.

"In an organized fashion" is putting it mildly. My husband is the master list-maker. His "To do" lists are longer and more detailed than many pieces of federal legislation. (One of his lists actually included the entry "Be nice to Lee" as a "to do" item!) The man owns no fewer than five different organizer "systems." He carries a voice memo recorder with him twenty-four hours a day, transcribes his verbal list at the end of the day, enters it into his computer memo file, and backs it up with two disks, a hard copy and a photostat. It's really sick.

The irony is he has no memory. I don't mean a bad memory, I mean no memory. He remembers nothing that has ever happened to him — not birthdays, not vacations, not surgical procedures. It's as if he has no past, as if he is born anew every morning. It is useless to begin a conversation with him with the words "Remember when . . ." because his stock and somewhat brusque reply is "No, I wasn't there." He won't even hear you out about which event you are asking him to remember. (He tripped himself up pretty good one time by insisting he "wasn't there" — the occasion I was referring to was our wedding.)

My elephantine memory has historically been a sore point between us, so he is taking no small delight in my recent lapses. He sees this as the perfect opportunity to introduce me to the world of leather-bound, mass-marketed time-management techniques, a move I have strenuously resisted in the past. He even went out and bought me my own big-deal organizer system and spent two hours training me how to use the various planning sections — you know, so I could learn how to make time my servant and be the master of my fate. (Am I the only one who thinks these time-management cults have totally lost perspective? I just want to remember to get razors and toothpaste. Couldn't these goals be accomplished with a seventy-nine-cent spiral notebook and a Bic pen?)

I couldn't bear to tell my husband that I didn't think I had the makings of a hard-core list-maker, so I tried to use the system for a couple of weeks. I really tried hard. I'd get up two hours early to fill out the exhaustive lists for each day's goals and objectives, but sometimes I still wouldn't get them finished. So, I'd skip lunch to catch up, but by the middle of the afternoon, I'd be too tired and hungry to do any of the things on my lists. I found myself sneaking out of bed in the middle of the night to fill in all of the sections that I had fallen behind on. Two weeks into the system, I still hadn't constructed an appropriate long-term personal-development plan, and I lived in constant fear that my husband would spring a surprise notebook check on me and discover that I was filling in Monday morning's lists on Wednesday night. It was a nightmare.

Then one morning I woke up with a very clear vision of what I needed to do. After my husband left for work, I dug out my old spiral notebook, opened it up to the first page and wrote down these few simple items:

1. Sell organizer system at garage sale.
2. Buy razors, stamps and two cans of corn.
3. Find Charlene Roddy and apologize in person.
4. Be nice to Bill.

I finally felt like the master of my fate. When my husband came home, I worked up the courage to show him my new list. I hung back while he read it. He was quiet for a few minutes and then he turned to me and said, "You really didn't need to put 'Be nice to Bill' on your list."

"Why not, because you can't live with an organizer reject like me any longer?" I asked, my voice trembling.

"No, because in the eighteen years we've known each other, you've never once forgotten to be nice to me," he replied and kissed me on the forehead.

And suddenly, without the aid of any organizer, list, or other contrivance, I remembered exactly why I had married him.

14

TAMING A WILD HAIR

I once began a term paper on the topic of human forgiveness with the sentence "What a wonderful and terrible thing is the power to forgive." I think most women feel the same way about their hair: What a wonderful and terrible thing is the power to grow hair. Short of the mother-daughter relationship, is there any other relationship that is so fraught with conflicting emotions as the one between a woman and her hair? Our hair is by turns our crowning glory and the bane of our existence. There is no more accurate a predictor of what kind of day a woman will have than the way her hair comes out in the morning. Not hormone levels, not financial status, not romantic prospects. The now clichéd phrase "bad hair day" reached its saturation point so quickly precisely because it resonated deeply with women from all walks of life.

Part of becoming a mature adult is making peace with the troubled relationships in your life, whether with your parents, your siblings, yourself, or, as in my case, your hair. Making peace with my hair has been a challenge because I don't have what you would call compliant hair. I don't have what you would call polite hair. I have big, bold, zest-for-living kind of hair, with a definite will of its own. It is hair that runs with wolves – and quite possibly descended from them. And having undergone every enlightenment process required of me as a responsible citizen of the '90s, I have learned not only to embrace my hair for who it is, but to actually revere it. In fact, I have exalted my hair to such a degree that at times I fear divine retribution for loving my hair more than God. Still, living with my hair can be exhausting. It's kind of like walking around with Luciano Pavarotti sitting on your head — an incredible energy force, but a bit hard to rein in.

I have always known about the duplicitous nature of my hair. In the early days before my great hair epiphany (which coincided with such advances in hair technology as confixor, molding gel and the diffuser), I hated my hair. The truth was, in my adolescent ignorance I didn't understand it. It wasn't like other hair. In other words, despite the fact that it was 1972, my hair stubbornly refused to go straight, lie flat or be parted down the middle. Every once in a while I would coax it into a middle part and manage to restrain it with these really nifty green barrettes long enough to pass through the admission desk at the Youth Center. Then I would confidently hit the dance floor with my friends, only to find out during a bathroom break (i.e., a slow song) that my newly tamed hair had viciously turned on me somewhere in the middle of "Green Eyed Lady." (My puny little barrettes were no match for a steamy dance hall full of teenagers.)

One of the first people who taught me to love my hair was the eminent hair surgeon Mr. Raymond from Mr. Raymond's House of Hair in Charleston, West Virginia. Mr. Raymond believed in taking a firm hand to unruly hair. "Your hair is like a child acting out to get attention," he explained to me at my first appointment. "It is begging for discipline and that's what I will give it. Not abuse, but discipline." Mr. Raymond was a tough taskmaster, ordering my hair to alternately smooth and fluff on his command. He worked my hair, and, wonder of wonders, my hair responded. Stubborn cowlicks capitulated. Wayward waves relaxed and fell submissively into place under his unyielding touch.

As a professional, Mr. Raymond was committed to providing excellent care to all hair, but I think he took a particular interest in mine because in a weird way he identified with it. Mr. Raymond knew what it was like to be different, to be misunderstood. I knew that Mr. Raymond was deeply grieved that no one in his family – certainly not his brother, the Pentecostal preacher — understood his penchant for wearing gold lamé evening gowns to places where such attire would seem to be inappropriate, such as Taco Bell. "They have no appreciation for the painful body waxing I endure to pull off this look," he once lamented to me in a private moment. "I'm trying to bring a little laughter to the world, but all they can do is criticize." Then putting on his professional hair-surgeon face, he twirled the curling iron through my hair and added, "But here I have created a masterpiece — championship-quality hair. Let's see anyone criticize this!"

I was proud that Mr. Raymond held such a personal investment in my hair, but I was afraid I wouldn't be able to live up to his high expectations. Inevitably, of course, I let him down. At the time I was hosting a local TV talk show, and Mr. Raymond took special pride in seeing his creation in the (rather limited) spotlight. Unfortunately, an extremely virulent strain of flu hit the area that winter, and I fell victim to it. I was the kind of sick where your only hope is that death will come quickly. I had been flat on my back for four days when my boss called and reminded me of a critical interview we had scheduled weeks before. He begged me to come in just long enough to do it because postponing would have derailed a month's worth of programming. I dragged myself out of bed and made it to the studio with exactly enough time to walk straight onto the set and begin the interview. As soon as the interview was over, I promptly fainted and was driven home. The last thing I was thinking about was how my hair looked.

Days later when I saw the final edited tape, I almost fainted again. Hair by Cuisinart, with an unusually lustrous sheen, compliments of Vick's Vapo Rub, would be one way to describe the 'do I was sporting. I couldn't believe anyone had let me go on camera like that. "We were really desperate to get this interview on tape," the director said by way of explanation. My hair looked so atrocious that people I didn't even know stopped me in the grocery store to comment on it. Once, when my mother was babysitting my daughter, a woman called and asked for me. When she learned I wasn't at home, she had the nerve to ask my mother, "So, what was the deal with her hair the other day?" Some people definitely have too much free time on their hands.

But the insensitive comments of strangers were nothing compared to what I knew would be the Wrath of Raymond. Mr. Raymond had been out of town since the night the interview aired, and I was dreading his return. The closer it got, the more panicky I became. Even so, even with my fear of our encounter in the forefront of my mind, Mr. Raymond struck unexpectedly. The night before he was due back, I was walking through the mall, lost in thought, when I was startled by someone yanking on my collar from behind. Instantly, my stomach leapt into my throat — I recognized that yank. I froze in my place. A quick survey of escape routes proved disappointing. It was six P.M. in the food court, a mob of hungry shoppers stood between me and the escalator. I was trapped. I had little choice but to turn around and stand face to face with my accuser.

"Way-ell," said Mr. Raymond with his strong West Virginia twang, taking a long drag on his Virginia Slims menthol. "I turned on the Tee-Vee the other night, and there you were. My Gaaaawwwwd, woman, your hair looked like hay-ell! I said to Devon, 'I do the woman's hair, but I did not do thay-at!'" He punctuated every last syllable by poking his lit cigarette in my face. As they say in West Virginia, he seemed mad enough to spit. I immediately began blubbering my mea culpas, whimpering like a scolded puppy.

"Oh, quit your crying, girl. You know I can't abide runny mascara," said Mr. Raymond, softening and putting his arm around my shoulder. He steered me to an empty table at the edge of the food court and pressed a wad of Kleenex into my hand. By the time he polished off a double order of cheese fries and a Strawberry Julius, he had forgiven me. I was so relieved. And, you know, in a way, I think he was glad that I had humiliated myself on camera because it was a testimony to how much he was needed in the world, gold lamé and all. The three of us — Mr. Raymond, my hair and I — remained on the best of terms until I moved away two years later.

Given my illustrious hair history, is it any wonder that I wrestled so mightily with the major midlife question of whether or not to color my encroaching gray last year? (As you remember, I put the kibosh on my sister's attempt to shave off all my gray hair.) Coloring my hair was not an action I could undertake lightly. The relationship between my hair and me had continued to grow and deepen since those first tentative days of our courtship under Mr. Raymond's tutelage. We had worked really hard to gain each other's trust and respect. Frankly, I was a little afraid of how my hair would react if I suddenly up and dumped a bottle of Warm Chestnut all over it. Would my hair interpret that as a sign that I no longer found it attractive? Would it think I was lusting after younger, more pigmented hair? And, most important, would it retaliate against me? For despite our hard-won mutual admiration, my hair was still very temperamental at heart. I knew my lush, bouncy locks could turn into a life-sized Chia Head faster than you could say "humidity index." Just the previous Wednesday — a really muggy day — I had flown to Chicago and had been forced to purchase a companion ticket to accommodate my hair. (Luckily, we were able to get two seats together.)

After nearly two years of gentle nudging from my stylist — who, with all due respect to Mr. Raymond, wields a pretty wicked round brush herself — I agreed to a color consultation. She was very patient with me, carefully explaining the protocol for each of the different procedures. "We are able to offer patients, er, clients, so many more options today than in our mothers' day," she said enthusiastically. "The technology is quite amazing."

After a thorough evaluation of my goals and an assessment of my risk factors, she determined that I was a good candidate for shading. I liked that idea because somehow shading didn't sound as serious, or as fraudulent, as outright dyeing. I decided I would do it. She gave me a stack of literature and a consent form and made an appointment for me for two weeks later.

In the meantime I was determined to educate myself about the procedure. I read all the information I could get my hands on and solicited second, third, and fourth opinions from everyone from master colorists at competing salons to the UPS man. Sometimes I would get excited about taking the plunge, but other times I would hyperventilate and be consumed with bad hair thoughts. I kept having visions of the time my sister dyed her hair illegally (i.e., against my mother's strict orders) in our bathroom when I was about seven years old. I don't know what kind of witch's brew she had whipped up, but when she rinsed it out, large clumps of hair came out with it. The image of that blue-black stew of hair circling our bathtub drain was burned into my mind.

Other times, I would have flashbacks of the "Dick Van Dyke" episode where Rob puts a salad dressing concoction on his hair and as a result has dreams that he A) goes bald or B) grows a head of lettuce. And his hair wasn't nearly as vindictive as mine could be. I called my stylist.

"I'm really nervous. You'll have to put me under or I won't make it through the procedure," I pleaded.

"Now, Lee, we talked about this. Shading does not require general anesthesia," she said deliberately.

"Well, if you won't put me under, at least give me a sedative beforehand," I begged.

"I'm afraid I can't do that," she said calmly.

"But this is me we're talking about. I need morphine just to get my eyebrows waxed," I countered.

"Well, you could always try breathing exercises to help you relax," she offered.

"Breathing exercises?" I screamed, incredulous. "I'm about to undergo the most delicate procedure in my hair's life, a procedure that may well provoke a violent and uncontrollable frizzing reaction that *I*, not *you*, will have to live with, and you want me to just breathe through it? That's barbaric!"

"Look," she said. "It's normal to feel some apprehension beforehand, but you really have nothing to worry about. I've done this procedure a thousand times, and the product we're using is very gentle. Trust me, your hair will love it. Afterall, it's the hair color that thinks it's a conditioner," she said with assurance.

"The hair color that thinks it's a conditioner?" I squawked. "That's supposed to make me feel better? My hair is crazy enough. The last thing I need is a coloring agent with multiple personalities."

"Lee, eat a KitKat. Everything will be fine, I promise," she said gently and hung up the phone.

Well, I am now a true believer in the miracles of modern hair science. My hair came through beautifully. No frizz, no fuzz. And the shading procedure was not only painless, it was over so quickly I didn't even get to finish reading the house copy of *Marie Claire*. (Now I'll never know the details of reader Micki B.'s most embarrassing sexual situation.) And I don't know about you, but I sleep better at night knowing that some of the greatest scientific minds of our time are dedicated to bringing us better living through hair technology. Vanity science, that's where it's at as far as I'm concerned.

As I was walking out the door of the salon with my newly shaded coiffure, I bumped into a male stylist I'd never seen before. Passing by me, he fairly squealed, "My Gaaawwwd, your hair looks good. I'd be proud to say I did thay-at!" I stopped dead in my tracks. The unshaded hair on the back of my neck stood on end. Can't be, I thought. No way. I turned to get a better look at him.

"Raymond?" I ventured cautiously.

"No, darlin', I'm Brian. I don't think we've met. I just moved down here from West Virginia."

"From West Virginia, you're kidding?"

"No, ma'am, I was born and raised there," he answered lightly.

I knew it was a long shot, but I just had to ask. "You're going to think this is a crazy question," I said. "But how do you feel about gold lamé?"

"About what?" he asked.

"Oh, never mind," I replied. "But I'm really glad you like my hair. Thanks."

Walking to my car, I couldn't help but think that somewhere in the world at this very moment there was a man in a gold lamé evening gown smiling to himself as he pulled up to the Taco Bell drive-thru window.

15

GIRLS' NIGHT OUT

The power of music is a frightening thing. Music's ability to evoke a mood, recreate a time, or suspend good judgment in otherwise sensible people is shockingly potent. Most of the dangerous/embarrassing things I have done in my life have been because the music I was listening to at the moment was either so exhilarating that I believed I was invincible or because it was so depressing that I believed I had nothing to live for anyway. I am so easily swayed by music that sometimes I scare even myself. My husband is fond of saying that it is safer for me to drink and drive than it is for me to listen to music and drive. And he knows whereof he speaks. He once stood out in the middle of the street frantically waving and shouting at me to get my attention as I blithely drove right by him. Hey, "Baby Love" was on. (Too bad for him it wasn't "Stop! In the Name of Love.")

If listening to music by myself is risky business, listening to music with a group of other women battling midlife malaise is almost lethal. One Saturday, a friend of mine brought a CD of great dance music with her to the gym. That hardly sounds daring or revolutionary now, but for some reason the music affected our little group in a profound way that day. Maybe it was because it was the first gorgeous day of spring after a long, dreary winter. The kind of day that demands that you get up and do something. Maybe it was because we had all been taking Vitamin E for the past several months. Maybe it was because our heavy sweats had given way to sleeker, more revealing bodywear. I can't explain the serendipitous confluence of elements that created the charge in the air that day; I only know that we all felt it. By the time Chaka Khan released the last suggestive note of "I Feel For You," smoke was coming out of our treadmills. Chaka seemed to provide just the spark we needed to ignite the youthful fire that we all secretly feared had been smothered under layers of wife/mom propriety.

"Boy, remember going out, listening to music, dancing all night?" said Diane wistfully.

"I was just thinking that," I said. "It used to be so much fun."

"Yeah, it really was," said Lisa.

We were all quiet for a minute, each of us taking a spin on her own mental dance floor, no doubt.

"But I still go out and listen to music," Linda sputtered defensively. "Almost every Saturday."

"Linda, the Chuck E. Cheese house band doesn't count," I said.

Lisa broke into song: "You say it's your birthday, it's my birthday too, yeah." Then she said, "You want to hear something pathetic? I've been listening to Fatz and Mindy sing that for so long that when I heard the real thing on the radio one day, my first thought was, 'Oh, the Beatles covered that?'"

"That's pretty sad," I said. "I'm glad I'm past the Chuck E. Cheese stage, but I know how you feel. Whenever I catch

'The Big '80s' on VH-1, I always expect them to play Raffi. That's what I was listening to during those years."

"All right, I can't take this anymore," said Diane. "We are going to do something wild. Our husbands are gone; we're having a girls' night out."

"But we've done that before," said Linda.

"This will be different," Diane said forcefully. "This time we're really going out. Somewhere fun. Somewhere where booster seats are illegal."

"Without a drive-thru window," said Lisa.

"And no all-you-can-eat salad bar," I said emphatically.

"Wow, where is such a place?" wondered Linda aloud.

"Out there, girls," I said, dramatically pointing out the window. "Out there is a place where loud music pulsates into the night. Where hip, trendsetting men throw their heads back laughing at with-it, trendsetting women who flip their hair forward in response. All that and more is waiting for us, out there. Beyond . . . the suburbs!"

We ran into the locker room gushing our plans for the evening. There was so much to do. Child care to secure, Kid Cuisines to microwave and under-eye sun damage to reverse, all in less than six hours. First, we put in a call to Maureen, our contact in the single world, to find out the current hot spot. The Canyon Club, hands down, she told us. It was decided that we would all meet at my house to put on our finishing touches and, at Linda's strong urging, to pick out fictitious names for the evening. She said it would lend an air of mystery to us, but I suspected it had more to do with safeguarding her reputation among the other den mothers.

"You're afraid the other Cub Scout mothers will catch wind of your wild night on the town, huh?" I asked teasingly.

"No, that's not it at all," she insisted. "Besides, I've told you a thousand times, it's not Cub Scouts, it's *Weblos* — We'll Be Loyal Scouts — Weblos! Cub Scouts were last year. Everybody knows that."

She was quiet for a minute and then said, "Oh, I'm sorry, but those Weblos mothers can be so cruel. They've been gunning for me ever since I accidentally set fire to the stupid tee-pee during Frontier Days last year. But I really have always wished my name were Rachael."

"Then Rachael it is," we all said in unison.

Our next hurdle was deciding who would drive. Acting as if they had been tipped off in advance, our husbands had taken all the cool cars to the airport, leaving us with slim pickings indeed. Linda's and Lisa's minivans with integral car seats were definitely out of the question — talk about defeating our purpose — and even Diane's station wagon seemed to scream Motherhood. We finally settled on my sedate sedan because, while not particularly cool, it was at least mercifully free of any "My Child Is A Good Citizen" bumper stickers.

Okay, we were making progress: We would go in my car, we would go to the Canyon Club and we would look stunning. "Or as stunning as I can while wearing a nursing bra," said Linda/Rachael, a mom for the third time at thirty-nine. "Do you think anyone will know?"

"Just don't wear your La Leche League T-shirt," I said.

When the group assembled at my house that evening, I had to admit we looked pretty hot. Not a PTA member in the group. We finalized our plan of attack. We would pick up Maureen at her place in town, head to the Canyon Club and then dance with total abandon into the wee hours. Well, until almost 11:30 anyway. Our original plan to stay out all night had developed a few glitches. Like Missy, Linda's thirteen-year-old babysitter, couldn't stay out past midnight. Like Miss Diane's Sunday school class, "the thumbsuckers," would be using scissors the next morning so she would need to have her wits about her. Like my husband who was in California would be calling me about midnight our time, and I couldn't fall asleep unless I talked to him. Thus we had to amend our curfew to 11:30 P.M. "But it will be quality wild time just the same," Diane insisted.

We ran down our final checklist: cell phones, pagers, fake names and a palette of the "New Nudes" lip colors. We were ready to take our show on the road. Ladies and gentlemen, presenting the entertainment extravaganza you've all been waiting for: "Girls' Night Out," starring Diane as Blake, Linda as Rachael, Lisa as Felicia, Lee as Francesca and Jerry Mathers as the Beaver.

As we pulled out of my driveway, I launched my special surprise. I hit the CD player and "Born To Be Wild" boomed out of the speakers to the squealing delight of my fellow wild women. I hit the CD player again, and in a matter of seconds, we were hanging our perfectly coiffed heads out the car windows, singing along in full agreement with Jimmy Buffett: "Fins to the left, fins to the right, and we're the only bait in town." This was going to be such a great night, I just knew it. We picked up Maureen and headed to the Canyon Club.

"What do you mean you have to leave at 11:30?" Maureen asked aghast. "Things don't even get started 'til about eleven."

"Then why are we going there now?" asked Lisa.

"We're not. I thought we were going to eat first," said Maureen.

"Look, I don't want to waste time eating when we only have a few hours to be wild women. I want to go straight to the club and start dancing," said Diane.

"Nobody goes there this early," said Maureen.

"Nobody?" I asked.

"Oh, excuse me, I'm sorry. Nobody except Nick the Crooner, a sixty-year-old ex-lounge singer who keeps telling me I'm 'a real dish,' and Shamir, a 5'2" Persian rug dealer from Tampa."

Just then Linda's cell phone rang. It was the babysitter. She couldn't get the baby to stop crying. Hearing the baby cry in the background was all the stimulus Linda needed. Geysers of milk were shooting everywhere. In her excitement, Linda had apparently forgotten to stop and buy nursing pads.

"Good grief, didn't you empty those things before you left home?" asked Maureen.

"Yes," said Linda. "But, I've just got a lot of milk."

"Well, don't aim 'em at me, Elsie," said Maureen impatiently.

"Quit picking on her and help me find something to stop up the leak," said Diane.

I concentrated on keeping us from getting killed in Saturday night downtown traffic while everyone else frantically searched their purses for suitable packing material. With two minipads in place in her bra, Linda regained her composure enough to instruct the babysitter how to calm the baby. We pulled into a poorly lit Burger King parking lot to give everyone a chance to recover. We quieted down just in time to hear the sickening sound of glass crunching under my rear tires. "I don't even believe this," I said, my head slumping against the steering wheel.

From what we could tell in the dark parking lot, my tire had not gone flat. We didn't spend too much time appraising the situation because the offers of "help" we were attracting were a little scary. We pulled out and finally headed to the Canyon Club to get this night back on track. When we got there, it seemed as if the Girls' Night Out goddesses were smiling on us at last because there was a nice crowd at the club even though it was well before eleven P.M. "It looks like our luck is changing," said Lisa.

Of course, that was before we got close enough to see the yellow crime tape. Contrary to what Maureen thought, some exciting things did happen at the Canyon Club in the early evening hours. Just ask the undercover DEA agents who were there. I never got the whole story — something about a sting operation and an unexpected exchange of gunfire — but obviously, the Canyon Club was off limits for the night, which was a shame because it did look like a neat place. The general consensus of the crowd of rubber neckers that had gathered in the parking lot was that we would all go down a few blocks to Frazzled, a newly opened, "high energy" dance club. "Whatever," said Lisa, pretty much summing it up for all of us. Our group now included Nick the Crooner, who was on us like white on rice as soon as he saw Maureen with us. "She's a real dish," he confided to me on the way over to Frazzled.

Frazzled is putting it mildly. There must have been four thousand sweaty bodies packed into a space designed for twelve. (Why is there never a building-code inspector around when you need one?) Not that I could have provided an accurate head count since the smoke was so thick I could barely see my hand in front of my face. Which is exactly where I had to keep it most of the time in order to hold Shamir, our height-challenged rug dealer friend, at bay. The guy came up to my chest, a situation that I did not find nearly as desirable as he did.

And the so-called music was nothing more than static amplified to the decibel level of a space shuttle launch. I knew I had no right to expect dance music from my era. I understood that no one besides me gave a hoot whether Alicia Bridges loved the nightlife or not. But after an hour of being Frazzled, I was desperate to hear something I recognized as music. Cheryl Crow, the Spice Girls, someone, anyone, vaguely familiar. And with drinks a whopping eight bucks apiece — four for club soda, a dollar extra for lime — there was no danger of my losing my status as the designated driver.

Linda and I finally made our way out to the porch where Lisa had become embroiled in a deep conversation about mythological archetypes with some horn-rimmed, mad scientist–type guy who looked like he and Medusa shared the same hairdresser. He displayed that distinctive combination of weird smartness and bizarre looks so characteristic of your more notorious serial killers. "Hey, Lisa, are you ready to go?" we asked.

"Yeah, I guess so," she answered, turning to us.

"Is your name Lisa?" asked the serial killer.

"Yes," she said without hesitation.

"But you said it was Felicia," he said angrily, slamming his fists down onto the table. "I thought we were talking absolute truths here, *Lee-sa*. I trusted you, and now I find out I've been deceived." He was becoming very agitated, starting to snort, actually.

"Oh, no, you haven't been deceived," Lisa quickly assured him. "My name is Felicia. And Lisa too. It's Lisa Felicia," she said without blinking.

"Lisa Felicia?" he asked, unconvinced.

"Yeah, you know, like Lisa Marie, Elvis's daughter," I interjected nervously. "Well, bye, we gotta go now," I said, pulling Lisa Felicia back inside.

We rounded up Diane — Maureen wanted to stay — and

left. Nick the Crooner (who wanted to pump us for information on Maureen) walked us to the car, a move he regretted as soon as we discovered the flat rear tire. "I guess it was a slow leak," said Linda. It was also a slow change. I've never seen anyone huff, puff and sweat so much changing a tire as Nick the Crooner. I also realized it was the first time all night that he wasn't humming "That's Amore" under his breath. With our tire changed, we departed, leaving Nick the Crooner standing alone in a pool of sweat.

Nobody said a word for about five miles. Finally, I said, "Lisa Felicia?!" Everyone started laughing.

"Do you think we're failures as wild women?" asked Linda.

"Definitely not. We're modified wild women, that's all," said Diane.

"That makes me feel better," said Linda.

"Still, I can't believe our big night out was a field trip to a crime scene," I said.

"Which one do you mean, the Canyon Club or Frazzled?" asked Lisa sarcastically.

"Oh, that Frazzled place was criminal," said Diane.

"Especially the drink prices," I said.

"Not to mention I couldn't breathe with all that smoke," added Linda.

"Well, it was certainly no place for a lactating mother," I agreed. "And they call that stuff they were playing music?"

"No kidding," said Lisa. "Hey, turn Jimmy Buffett back on."

"Cheeseburger in Paradise" came on, and perfectly on cue, we all said, "I'm starving!"

"Go to the Wendy's by my house," said Linda.

"I thought it closed at ten," said Lisa.

"Not the drive-thru. That's open 'til midnight. We can

get pretty wild out here in the 'burbs sometimes."

Going to Wendy's sounded like the best idea we'd had all night. But first we stopped at Kroger so Linda could get a box of nursing pads. We all went into the store with her. We were still lamenting our botched up evening when a funny thing happened. Strolling the aisles of Kroger we realized that KRGR, the in-store radio station, was playing really good music. Earth, Wind and Fire in produce, Fleetwood Mac in frozen foods, the Beatles in the deli. They even had good food samples left. Pretty soon we were all singing, dancing and eating our way through the wide, spacious aisles.

"This is fantastic," said Diane. "This is just what we were looking for. Familiar music in a clean, safe, well-lit environment."

"Plus free food," said Lisa.

"Plus cute bag boys," I said.

"Plus double coupons," added Linda.

"Well, my fellow modified wild women," I said with a keen sense of satisfaction, "it just doesn't get any better than this."

And on that particular Saturday night, we all agreed that truer words had never been spoken.

16

BY THEIR FEET SHALL YE KNOW THEM

I had planned to make my entree into midlife by putting my best foot forward. To do that, however, I would likely have to borrow someone else's feet. I may still have youth in my soul, but old age has crept into my metatarsals. My feet hurt. A lot. My husband has added "Are you wearing comfortable shoes?" to the verbal checklist he runs through each time we leave the house nowadays. It's so humiliating. Why doesn't he just yell out, "Ma, did get your teeth out of the glass?" for the whole neighborhood to hear? Forget counting the rings on a tree. For my money, the most effective gauge of aging is the progression (regression?) of women's footwear as the years pass. From three-inch spike-heeled slingbacks to more forgiving, but still stylish, flats to sneakers with gel insoles, my foot fashion quotient is falling faster than my arches.

I don't think I put it too strongly when I say that for most women, to have shoes is to have life. Every woman I know — young or old, short or tall, thin or not-so-thin — loves shoes. We consider shoes the true foundation garment because without good ones, we're not going anywhere. Admit it, despite our rightful public outrage and disgust at the excesses of Imelda Marcos back in the '80s, wasn't there just some teeny-weeny little private part of us that said, "God help me, but I kind of understand her shoe thing"?

It's not our fault. Love of shoes is encoded on our DNA in much the same way that love of TV remote controls is encoded on men's. We don't have a chance. As soon as we are born, our mothers, grandmothers and aunts conspire with nature to ensure our successful development into full-fledged shoe hogs. They buy us tiny infant footwear so darling that even a roomful of the most level-headed, serious-minded women — women who can calculate compound interest in their heads — have been known to squeal, "These shoes are sooooo cuuuuuuuuute!" at the mere sight of a pair of miniature terry cloth sandals. Or a pair of itsy-bitsy pink moccasins. Or, the killer for me, little suede clogs with foam rubber soles. Of course, none of these shoes serves any practical purpose whatsoever, the chances of your average three-month-old taking a stroll around the block under her own steam being very slim. No wonder we are in such a rush to toddle over to mom's closet and slip into that pair of blue marabou-trimmed mules.

When I was about four years old, I wanted this pair of little kids' plastic high heels from the toy aisle at the A&P in the worst way. I wanted them more than a Tiny Tears doll, more than that baby bottle that looked like it had real milk in it. In my estimation, Dorothy's ruby slippers didn't have half the cachet of these $2.49 plastic shoes. I was completely capitivated by the idea of kid-scaled high heels. I mean, it was one thing to play dress-up clomping around in my mother's obviously too big shoes, but to play dress-up wearing my very own high heels, shoes that were practically custom made for my kid-sized foot, well, just the thought of it made me giddy with independence.

I never got those shoes, but I never stopped dreaming about them. Then on the very first day of kindergarten, a wonderful thing happened. Our teacher, Mrs. Fisher, was showing us the different areas of the classroom — blocks, dollhouse, instruments — and when we got to the playhouse area, there they were, in the box marked "Mommy clothes." My shoes, the very ones that I had been coveting for the past year. When Mrs. Fisher said that all the girls could take turns wearing them, I was delirious with happiness. I was going to love kindergarten. Every afternoon for the rest of the year, I waited patiently for my turn to wear the Mommy shoes, for my turn to be transported to the heights of kindergarten sophistication. Cinderella could keep her glass slippers as far as I was concerned. For fifteen minutes every weekday, I had something even better. I had my own high heels.

If you think I'm overemphasizing the power of shoes as a touchstone in your life, try this test with me. I'll name a shoe style, and you think of all the images that it brings to your mind.

First pair of pumps: About seventh grade, right? And if your Mom let you get pumps, that meant you were finally allowed to wear "nylons" which, of course meant you had also secured permission to shave your legs and possibly wear Bonne Bell lip gloss in honor of your having breached the threshold of womanhood by either getting your period or possibly making your confirmation.

Wedgies: Remember this versatile footware? They looked equally good (?) with minis, midis, and hot pants. And if you were wearing wedgies on your feet, you don't have to tell me that you were wearing a suede choker around your neck and either Love's Lemon or Love's Baby Soft on your wrists, you hipster, you.

Platforms: I don't care how ridiculous these shoes actually were (or continue to be in their '90s incarnation), I loved this style. Was there any other shoe that made your legs look as long, that could make even me look almost tall? On the other hand, there was probably no other shoe style that all but guaranteed that you would end up in traction. Still, I found platforms, a peasant dress, and a shag haircut to be a formidable fashion combo.

Ballet slippers: Worn with black opaque tights, coordinating bodysuit and a denim wrap skirt, they were the shoes of choice for all female college artistes who wrote bad confessional poetry and self-consciously acted in the moment on various black-box stages around campus. Oh, the angst, the utter Sturm und Drang of it all.

Candies: Oh, leave the tortured artistes in their lofts, honey, they are way too serious. Get yourself a pair of Candies and Gloria Vanderbilt jeans, and let's strut our stuff. I say we make a night of it at places with names like The Giraffe and The Library and bring it home to the sounds of Chic at The Landing Strip. Buckle your safety belts!

See, told ya! Shoes have added immeasurable richness to the fabric of our lives over the years. Looking back now, it's hard for me to pinpoint exactly when I began the slow slide into this latest and most dreaded stage of my shoe-wearing life — the comfortable-shoe stage. (Which is about a shoelace breadth's away from the hideous "sensible shoe" stage.) I do recall that for several months as far back as 1979 — a few weeks following a half-off sale on gorgeous leather cowboy boots —I suffered a wicked bout of little toe pain.

All day long, my cowboy-booted little toes would feel like someone was pressing a two-thousand-pound anvil on them. The only thing that hurt worse than this constant pressure was the sudden removal of that pressure when I took off my boots at the end of the day. I couldn't simply kick off my boots and free my toes all at once, the pain would be too intense. I would have to gently ease each foot out of its respective boot and squeeze my little toes firmly between my thumbs and forefingers gradually massaging them out of captivity over a fifteen-minute period. It was quite a ritual, one that I didn't particularly care to share with my handsome new boyfriend. I would dance with him for hours in excruciating pain because I couldn't picture myself casually tossing off something like, "Hey, Babe, I gotta sit this one out, my dogs are killin' me."

I knew what the problem was, but it seemed too old, gross, and disgusting-sounding a condition to afflict someone of my tender age. After a few months of painful denial, I broke down and went to the podiatrist.

"You have some good-sized corns here, Lee," he said.

And to think I had actually been worried that I'd planted my crops too late that year.

"You've got to get them taken care of or they'll get even bigger," the doctor continued.

"You mean like 'Knee high by the Fourth of July'?" I asked, only half-kidding.

"Well, something like that. But we do have to take care of them."

"Will this treatment involve the use of contour plowing?" I asked.

"No," he laughed.

"This is so nasty," I said. "Only old women with rolled-down support hose get corns."

"No, young women who buy fashionable footwear with inadequate toe boxes get corns," he corrected me.

"Can we at least not use the term 'corn'?" I asked.

"What would you prefer?"

"How about 'maize'?" I suggested.

I came clean with my boyfriend when I got home, and instead of shunning me as an untouchable or even laughing in my face, he said sympathetically, "You poor thing, why didn't you tell me? I would have rubbed your feet for you." (I booked the church and reception hall immediately!)

So I went with more ample toe boxes and escaped any corn-related complications for the next several years. Then a couple of years ago, I started feeling like a sharp stone was digging into the ball of my foot every time I put weight on it. Again, I went to the foot doctor. If you think it was hard for me to take the corn diagnosis, you should have heard me gag when I found out I had produced a plantar's wart.

"A plantar's wart?" I asked disdainfully. "Well, it figures. Plant corn, get a plantar's wart."

"Excuse me?" said the doctor.

"Never mind," I said. "Just do what you gotta do."

Well, he lasered that baby out right then and there. And let me tell you, there's nothing like the smell of your own flesh being vaporized to buoy up your spirits during a surgical procedure.

"That thing was huge," the doctor told me when he was finished.

I think he intended that as a compliment, but I felt less than flattered.

"Now about your bunion," he started as the nurse was bandaging my foot.

"My what?" I shrieked. "I do not have a bunion. I'm not even forty yet; I flat-out refuse to have a bunion."

"No, you don't actually have a bunion," he said quickly. "But you could be headed for one if you don't start wearing more appropriate footwear. And let me ask you," he continued, "do your feet feel tired and achy a lot of the time?"

"Yes, my husband is sick to death of rubbing them," I said. (Seventeen years of marriage have understandably worn thin his promise to nurse my hurting feet.)

"Well, that's your badly fallen arches," he explained. "Your feet are virtually flat and you really should be wearing a custom-molded arch-support appliance in your shoes at all times."

This was too much information for me to absorb. I was picturing how attractive my new strappy sandals would look with a custom-molded arch-support *appliance* shoved into them.

"This is very hard news for someone who has made feet the focal point of her life," I said.

"I suspect what you mean to say is that you have made your shoes, not your feet, the focal point of your life. Like most women, you take your feet for granted. You expect your feet to accommodate your shoes, when it should be the other way around," he said shaking his head and clucking his tongue.

I felt like I had killed someone. "Oh, I guess you're right, Doctor," I sighed. "There is blood on my hands, not to mention my feet. What can I do about it now?"

He sat down with me and together we worked out a reasonable foot-care program designed to provide me with many years of healthy foot usage.

Not too long ago, my husband surprised me with a day of pampering at a nearby spa. My special treatments included a forty-five-minute foot massage — heavenly — and a professional pedicure. I was nervous that my feet would betray me in public, but the pedicure passed without incident. The pedicurist seemed generally unfazed by the condition of my feet. (Except, that is, for my practice of "layering" toenail polish. You mean people actually bother to remove the old polish first? Even during the winter?) After applying the top coat, she gave me a pair of disposable plastic thongs to wear so I wouldn't smudge my polish. I flip-flopped my way across the parking lot to my car and drove home. When I got there, my husband was waiting to hear all about my "Queen For A Day" experience.

"It was great," I told him. "I picked up some new moves for you to try on my feet." He groaned.

"Even the pedicure was enjoyable," I continued. "And look, they gave me these neat little thongs to wear home so I wouldn't smudge my nail polish. I kind of hate to throw them out. They might come in handy for wearing in hotel showers or around the pool."

"Don't even think about it," said my husband. "Those are hardly regulation shoes for your feet," he said. "And I'll be the one stuck 'rubbing out' your mistake."

"Yeah, you're right," I agreed. "They're not exactly what you'd call arch-friendly footwear. Still, you gotta admit one thing," I added, taking the thongs off my feet.

"What's that," my husband asked.

"The toe boxes are wide open!"

17

TONGUE OF WAR

Some years ago when my daughter was first learning to read, my husband and I played the game Guesstures (it's like Charades) with her. When it was my daughter's turn, she selected a card, read it to herself and began acting out the phrase on it. She screwed up her face angrily and repeatedly thrust out her tongue at us. She wagged her tongue back and forth while vigorously shaking her finger at it. My husband and I had never seen such a display. We could not imagine what on earth was on the card she had picked. "Tongue-lashing? Tongue-whipping? Tongue-tied?" She shook her head "no" in response to each of our guesses and redoubled her efforts to contort her face and tongue. Finally, the clock ran out, and she collapsed onto the couch, exasperated with our inability to come up with the right answer. "What was it?" we cried.

"Tongue of War!" she exclaimed as if we were the biggest dopes in the world. "See," she said with satisfaction, showing us the card.

"What?" we asked confused, and then fell down laughing when we realized that to a beginning reader the phrase "tug of war" might easily be misconstrued as "tongue of war."

Maybe that incident implanted some kind of time-released subliminal message in my brain because the closer I get to forty, the closer I get to having my very own tongue of war, ready to strike at any and all rude, selfish, and pompous targets that cross my path. A lifetime built on polite conversation and carefully couched truths is coming unraveled before my eyes, and I don't think it's a minute too soon.

Maybe you will have a greater appreciation for how dramatic a change this is if I give you some background information. For example, I am the only woman I know who tacked a copy of the Act of Contrition to the wall of her labor room to use as a focal point. I sought forgiveness from God and the labor nurses for everything from not dilating fast enough to getting a leg cramp to having chapped lips. In fact, I spent more time apologizing than I did actually pushing. I am also the same woman who once fired a grossly incompetent cleaning woman (her idea of thorough cleaning was to flush the toilet after she threw her cigarette butts in it) with these harsh words: "Um, Louise, I was wondering if maybe you could not work here anymore. I mean, I'd continue to pay you every week, but, like, could you just not show up? Would that be okay?"

It's not that I didn't know what to say; it's just that I rarely had the nerve to say it aloud. That tendency to hold back has been weakening over the last few years, and strangely enough I think that having lived in West Virginia a while back laid the groundwork. When you live in West Virginia, you are forced to become verbally aggressive to defend yourself against the endless wisecracks your highfalutin', out-of-state friends make about you and your adopted home. ("So tell me, when a man and woman get divorced in West Virginia, are they still legally considered brother and sister?")

Here's a typical example of how to employ self-deprecating West Virginia humor to deflate your smart-alecky colleagues and acquaintances. When one of them asks you, with mock sincerity, if people in West Virginia wear shoes, you say, "Of course, we wear shoes. Geez, what do you think, we go back and forth to the outhouse in our bare feet?!"

That particular remark comes to us courtesy of my friend Pam, a native West Virginian with impeccable credentials — i.e., she has several double relatives, such as an aunt that's a cousin and an uncle that's a step-nephew. (Although I want to make it clear these cases are the result of marriage and that no blood lines have actually been crossed.) Pam was a good influence on me, and I did her proud. One day the two of us attended the grand opening of the local link of a national restaurant chain. One of the restaurant's representatives, who hailed from Waco, Texas, that cultural mecca, asked us what we thought of the Tex-Mex menu. Obviously kidding around, Pam and I answered with exaggerated Southern accents that we really liked those "fa-*gee*-tas," to which, Mr. Cosmopolitan patronizingly replied, "Actually, it's 'fa-*hee*-tas.'" Then he added, "But, of course, you couldn't know that, being from West Virginia." Without skipping a beat, I returned the phonics lesson with "Actually, it's 'West Vir-*hin*-ia.' But, of course, you couldn't know that, being a moron." Pam made me an honorary West Virginian for life that day.

In the years since then, my tongue of war and I have routinely sent overdressed salads back to the kitchen, returned poorly laundered shirts to the cleaners, and even given loud, drunken men at basketball games some much needed etiquette pointers. These small successes gave me the confidence I needed to tackle the big guys. Once, in the very same week, I told off a college president from South Georgia and the soon-to-be ex-wife of my husband's soon-to-be ex-colleague. The college president and I were making small talk at a professional gathering when he expressed disbelief at my ethnic heritage. "You are lying through your teeth," he said. "You can't be EYE-talian," he explained. "In the first place, you don't have any pock marks, and in the second place, you don't have hairy arms." I was so dumbstruck that I couldn't speak for a few seconds. Finally, I wrapped my hand firmly around his arm, looked him in the eye, and said in a very calm voice, "Sir, when I relay this conversation to my Uncle Vito, you'll wish to God I had been lying." I turned to walk away, then paused and looked over my shoulder at his feet. "What are you, about a 10 1/2 D? We like a snug fit, with no wasted cement," I said smiling and left the room.

I didn't know which infuriated me more, his unbelievable nerve or his frightening stupidity. If only I were Sicilian, I thought. Then I could at least give him the evil eye and make him grow horns or something. As a second-generation Piemontese, what could I do? Make his risotto come out runny for the rest of his life? (Big deal, add a little more cheese.)

The almost ex-colleague's almost ex-wife, Cindy, was much more fun. This woman was the most pretentious, superficial, self-absorbed, Land Rover-driving, Merlot-swilling, cut-out doll of a person I have ever met. The kind of woman whose idea of a witty retort is to say, "Isn't that just a hoooooot!" She weighed exactly 3 1/4 ounces (2 1/2 of which consisted of various hair colors) and sought sympathy from the rest of us all night long about her struggle against what she termed her "awful tendency to be such a lardo." She managed to keep herself in respectable condition, she told us, by "working out just bo-koo and bo-koo," but her husband, Frank, on the other hand, was a complete embarrassment to her. I mean, the guy had the nerve to weigh in right in the middle of the revised height-weight charts. Imagine! And sometimes he would work late — those pesky Land Rover payments nipping at his heels, no doubt — and not even go to the gym at all. "I hate to be seen with him he's gotten so hefty," she said. (She didn't mind being seen with his hefty checkbook, however.)

After spending a mere three hours with this woman, I couldn't believe that Frank was ever tempted to overeat. One evening with her was all it took to completely turn my stomach. When she shared the details of the latest plan that she and her friend Becky had devised to get Frank on the fast track to anorexia, I could feel the West Virginia impulse in me rising.

"We decided I would tell Frank that there would be no more romance until he got serious about working out," Cindy began. "The other night, when Frank started getting frisky, I said, 'Frank, there is no way I will allow your big flabby stomach to come in contact with my tight little tummy. If you want me, you're gonna have to start doing things differently from now on.' So, you know what he said then, don't you?" she said, winking at us.

"Roll over?" I offered innocently.

In the face of overwhelming laughter from every other woman in the room, Cindy reluctantly agreed that while that had not been her answer of choice, it was nonetheless, "a real hoooot!" (Frank quit his job and served her with divorce papers a few weeks after this party.)

But, you know how life is — just when you start to get a little too confident, you are brought low. My office, which consisted of four extremely talented women sharing one backbone among us, had become saddled with one of Murphy Brown's secretary rejects. We had done it to ourselves. This woman had been a casual acquaintance of ours, and we took pity on her because she was married to the biggest Neanderthal this side of the Pleistocene Age. The guy belonged in a glacier somewhere. (For example, he believed that most women could use a good dose of "dilapidary" – a.k.a dipilitory — cream, hairy broads being particularly offensive to his delicate sensibilities.) Turning my newly honed tongue of war loose on him would have only made life more miserable for Alex, his little woman. So, when we needed a secretary and Alex expressed interest in the job, we thought we would be doing our sisterly duty by hiring her.

Things didn't go quite as we had anticipated. It wasn't the fact that she had obviously lied about being able to spell, type or file — hey, we all have faults — it was more her little personality quirks that started to be a problem. Alex, who never said more than two words in the presence of Java Man, became a nonstop talking machine the second she walked through the office doorway every morning. (Okay, I talk a lot, but not when I'm working.) As the weeks wore on, her conversation developed this disconnected, stream-of-consciousness quality, punctuated by loud bursts of unrelated laughter.

Then there was her annoying habit of putting things in the wrong places. I don't mean putting the scissors in the top drawer instead of the middle one, I mean stabbing them point-down into the desktop.

Her behavior grew more and more bizarre until one morning she brought a pot of coffee into the conference room during a meeting and filled everyone's cup. As soon as we all took a sip, she gathered up all the cups and poured the coffee back into the pot saying, "Finder's keepers, loser's weepers." Suddenly, Java Man was starting to seem like the normal one.

I was elected to have a talk with her, my strong tongue of war being a thing of renown by now. She and I were in the car driving to lunch when I started to broach the subject of her odd behavior, with the eventual goal of firing her. I had barely begun to unfurl my mighty tongue when she interrupted me to tell me about the horrible fight she had had with her sister the night before.

"My sister wanted me to go to Wendy's! Can you believe that?!" Alex exclaimed.

"Um, no, I can't," I said, trying to sound supportive. "Are you trying to cut out fast food?"

"No!" she shouted. "Wendy's hamburgers are square!" She slammed her fists on the dashboard. "She knows I'm afraid of square hamburgers. She knows it! And she still tried to trick me into going there."

I decided pretty quickly that it might be wise to hold my fire for the moment. "That was really insensitive," I said sympathetically. "You know I would never do something like that."

"And she won't do it again either. She made me so mad," Alex said, turning to me. "I was really angry last night," she continued, almost panting. "I've never told you this, but I have kind of a problem with rage."

"You do? Oh, wow, who would've thought?" I said, trying to sound casual while mentally composing my will.

"She made me the kind of mad where everything just goes white, you know? Then it got real quiet, and I heard Dr. Gray's voice telling me, 'Alex, you always have a choice.' I said to myself, 'Alex, you can go get yourself a hammer and smash everything she owns, or you can eat a cherry Lifesaver,'" she said.

I was afraid to ask which course of action she had settled on.

"Dr. Gray is helping me make better choices," she added.

"I see," I said. "So, you're trying to learn less destructive ways of expressing your emotions?" I asked, trying to keep the conversation on a clinical level.

"Right!" she said. "Like, now, whenever I have the urge to set a building on fire, I chew gum instead. Sometimes a whole box of peppermint Chicklets — it has to be Chicklets."

"Well, of course," I said. "It would be absurd to rely on Wrigley's."

"Exactly!" she said gratified. "Have you been in therapy with Dr. Gray, too?"

"Soon," I said and realized with relief that I had managed to drive back to the office without her noticing.

"I just realized I forgot my checkbook," I said by way of explanation. "I'll be right back," I told her as I reached for the car door.

"Wait," she said, grabbing my arm. I stifled the urge to scream bloody murder, which wasn't easy, considering I was trapped in a car with a homicidal maniac, and all I had for protection was a half-empty pack of sugarless Bubble Yum. I promised God that if I got out alive, I would go directly to the Revco across the street and load up on Chicklets multi-packs. I would never leave myself this foolishly vulnerable again.

"Lee, I have something to tell you," Alex said soberly. I clenched my body against the blunt force trauma that was about to be inflicted upon it. "I'm quitting my job," she said.

I opened one eye. "You're quitting?" I repeated, thinking I must have heard wrong.

"Yes."

"Why?" I asked. Talk about looking a gift horse in the mouth.

"Well, don't take this the wrong way, but I'm having a hard time adjusting to everyone's personalities. You all are a little strange," she said apologetically.

I couldn't believe my ears, Chicklet Woman was calling *us* strange. Fortunately, my instinct for survival quickly overtook my bruised pride. "Oh, yes, you are so right," I agreed enthusiastically. "We are some of the strangest women I know. I don't blame you one bit for quitting. In fact, I can't believe you put up with us this long."

"No hard feelings?" she asked.

"Absolutely not," I said.

"Join me in a Chicklet?" she offered, taking a box from her purse.

"Thanks, I believe I could use one," I said.

Alex left my car and and our lives that very moment. We never heard from her again. Someone in her neighborhood later told me that Alex's husband had been transferred unexpectedly, and that they had moved lock, stock, and dilapidary cream to Minnesota. Alex may have been completely wacko, but she did teach me a very valuable lesson: Knowing when to hold your tongue of war is every bit as important as knowing when to unleash it. Chicklet, anyone?

18

SIMPLE PLEASURES

The hottest buzzword in baby boomer circles right now is "simplifying." I can't turn around without someone telling me I should be scaling back, cutting down, and returning to basics. After years of drowning ourselves in acquisitiveness, my generation has suddenly decided that the old Van Camp's Baked Beans commercial from the '70s was right — life's simple pleasures are the best. This trend is being touted as something of a cultural awakening, proof that we as a generation have finally become people of substance and have achieved the emotional maturity to understand what is really important in life. As appealing as the idea of simplifying our lives sounds, I am suspicious about what is really going on here. I mean, let's be honest. How realistic is it to think that the original "Me Generation" has suddenly adopted salt-of-the-earth values without ulterior motives? As a card-carrying member of that very generation, I'd have to say, "not very."

Don't get me wrong. I am all for simplification — especially regarding the application of sunless tanning products — but this particular '90s version seems fraught with contradictions. First of all, for something simple, it's pretty complicated. I mean, we can't just decide on our own to stop buying unnecessary luxury items or start valuing sunsets over elaborate custom-made window treatments. No, we must first read twenty-seven books, watch twelve videos and listen to at least four audiotapes to make sure we are doing it right. Of course, if we want to become true experts, we should attend the six-hour workshop, "Simplifying Your Life in 726 Easy Steps" conveniently offered at sites around the country for a reasonable $425. (Workbook and other materials priced separately.)

Getting serious about simplifying our lives also requires the proper wardrobe, namely tastefully accessorized "rugged wear" ensembles from Eddie Bauer, which are shown to their best advantage when worn driving our fully loaded, "earthy" Jeep Grand Cherokees on our way to eat at our favorite "rustic" lodge-themed restaurant. Hey, we are trying our darnedest to be simpler, more genuine people, but it's not easy for a generation who cut their teeth on Incredible Edibles to eschew the trappings of a consumer society.

But, you know what's really driving the compelling urge to return to simpler times? We are tired. "Simplifying" is boomer speak for "exhaustion." We take great pains to make our slower pace and lowered expectations seem intentional, but the truth is we are just too worn out to slay any more dragons. Middle age is the classic time for reevaluating goals and values and ultimately reconciling ideals with reality. For example, I often find myself reflecting on my life and concluding with satisfaction that while I have not become the ruler of several small nation-states as I had anticipated, my gumline has not receded at an overly alarming rate. All in all, life is good.

Simplifying, in this sense is a very good thing. Indeed, lowered expectations greatly enhance our chances for success and contentment as we enter midlife. I am a lot more realistic about my limitations now than when I was younger. For example, when I was in grade school, I used to set impossible goals for myself each Lent. I'd take a vow, doomed to certain failure, that I would not so much as make eye contact with an M&M for forty long days and nights. Now I tend to make Lenten or New Year's resolutions that run more along the lines of giving up sushi or Marilyn Manson concerts, things I know I can accomplish.

The idea of lowering, or at least altering, our expectations is endorsed by such diverse authorities as psychologists, time-management experts, and travel agents. Feeling in desperate need of a vacation, I fixed my focus on the altered-expectation spiel of the travel agent quoted in the "Living" section of the Sunday paper. "If you need a break, but don't have the time to take a full-blown vacation right now, don't overlook the wonders of a weekend getaway. If you can't escape to the Tuscan countryside, drink wine and eat pasta on the terrace of a country inn closer to home," she said. Surely she was speaking directly to me. Me, who could make eating pasta on a terrace an Olympic event. Me, whose husband's 187-hour workweek precluded a leisurely intercontinental excursion any time before the return of Hale Bopp. Perfectly anticipating my next move, the sidebar listed several charming inns around the country where my husband and I could recapture whatever it was we had lost — namely, the will to live — during the past year of stress overload. I picked one and began formulating my plans for our four-day restorative.

Let me say right from the outset that I played by the rules: I had almost no expectations whatsoever. In my opinion, the big selling points for the inn I had selected were that it was the out of the way, being located on an island in the middle of a large lake, and that there was almost nothing to do but lie in the sun and sleep. I don't think expectations can get too much simpler than that. Still, I hadn't counted on taking a one-and-a-half-hour flight, a thirty-dollar (plus tip) taxi trip, and a gut-churning ferry ride to reach our getaway destination only to be greeted by a woman wearing hot-pink stretch pants and a tube top, holding a vacuum cleaner in one hand and a lit cigarette in the other. I could hear my expectations scraping against the floor. Half of the place was completely boarded up (since about 1967 is my guess), and the other half should have been. Doris showed us to our room in the west wing. The Three Stooges never had a place that looked this bad. It had a Murphy bed, for crying out loud. Doris pulled down the bed and told us to be careful because one night she and Herb had gotten "jammed up pretty good in this contraption." Of course, that was before Herb's bypass surgery, she added. He was a "real humdinger" before the "klo-les-trol" got to him, she assured us.

After Doris left, my husband and I stood in stunned silence for a few moments. He then made a tour of the rest of our suite. I laid my magazine on the corner of the bed and sat down on top of my makeshift sterile field. Perfectly on cue, the bed collapsed under me. My husband came running out of the bathroom. As he helped me up from the floor he said, "We're not alone."

"What do you mean?" I asked.

"I counted eleven roaches on the bathroom counter," he said. "And they're not afraid of humans because they didn't even flinch when I turned on the light." (By which he meant he pulled the string attached to the bare lightbulb in the ceiling.)

"Great, pet roaches," I said. "Maybe we can get them to fetch our slippers for us."

— · —

"Well," said Doris shaking her head. "I don't understand what you don't like about the room. Herb and I were always very happy in #12, but maybe you'll find one of our beach cottages more to your taste."

She showed us to the beach cottage, which, while completely cruddy and disgusting, did have the advantage of a bed that did not originate in the wall, and a dilapidated front porch that caught the lake breezes, thereby helping to dissipate the pervasive stench of Doris's perpetually lit Lucky Strikes. There was no getting off the island before the next morning, so I was lowering my expectations by the minute.

"We'll take it," my husband and I said in unison.

"Okay," said Doris. "Now, about the rats — "

"The what?" I shrieked.

"The rats," Doris continued matter-of-factly. "You'll need to close the doors every day at 4:30, 4:45 at the latest, because that's the time of day they like to make their move indoors."

I couldn't even speak. Doris prattled on as if rats inviting themselves into your home were the most natural thing in the world.

"Now, if they do get in, just take care of them," she said, pointing to the corner where there sat a trap big enough to hold a chimpanzee.

My mind was reeling. First of all, I wondered, how precise was a rat's sense of time? If the door was standing open at, say, 4:28, would a gang of gutsy rats try to pull a fast one by sneaking in early? Conversely, would they bang on the door, angrily demanding access if I closed up shop before the deadline? Did they know about daylight savings time? And what exactly was involved in "taking care of them?" Did Doris mean to say that if we caught one, we had to feed and clothe it? If it was injured by the trap, did we have to pay for physical therapy? How about counseling to address its obvious problem with boundary issues? What exactly were our moral and legal obligations in providing "care" for a rat?

"How could they have recommended this place in the newspaper?" I asked incredulously after Doris left.

"I don't know," my husband said.

Just then, we heard a knock at our door. I grabbed my husband's wrist to check his watch. It was only 2:30. I would not be intimidated by some johnny-come-early rats. I was not letting them in; rules were rules. But our visitors turned out to be of the human variety. Bonnie, Burt, and their two-year-old son, Jason. They had been led astray by an article in a travel magazine and had arrived at "Paradise Lost" the day before. We were swapping war stories and planning our escape back to civilization when I heard scurrying noises on the porch.

"It's them," I screamed, automatically leaping onto a chair. But it wasn't them; it was only, in little Jason's words, "Rahoon." Rahoon was the probably rabid, definitely brazen raccoon that had held our comrades-in-arms hostage the previous afternoon while he rummaged around their deck, drinking half a wine cooler, lying on their beach towels and — get this — trying on Jason's sandals. "Well, he actually just stepped on them, but it looked like he was trying them on," Bonnie quickly explained. Hearing them go on about the great Rahoon, I half expected to look out the window and see an exotic creature wearing a turban, a precious jewel glinting in the middle of his furry forehead. As awful as this trip had been thus far, I thought it might almost have been worth it just to see Rahoon in all his swamilike splendor. But, dashed expectations once again. There was nothing exalted about Rahoon. He was a just a crummy old domestic raccoon.

—·—

"Just name your price," my husband said to Gus, the owner of the ferry service. "I don't care what it costs, we have to get back to the mainland tonight."

Burt and my husband were negotiating with Gus, who had closed down for the day, to get us back to civilization. Two hundred dollars later, the five of us were sloshing across the lake on the first leg of a journey that we hoped would land us all back safely in our own beds by midnight. "Rahoon bad!" Jason said emphatically as the island receded behind us. "Rahoon very bad," we all agreed.

By the time we disembarked from the ferry, tracked down a cab and arrived at the airport, the last flight had already left. But there was no stopping us. We forfeited our plane tickets, rented a car and drove all night long, arriving home eight A.M., exactly twenty-four hours after we had first left. Only a stiff back kept me from bending over and kissing the cement driveway. Home had never looked so good to me.

"I can't believe we have traveled by plane, taxi, ferry and rental car; encountered roaches, Rahoon and the threat of pushy rats; withstood the judgment of Doris, Gus, and the other natives, all to end up back home twenty-four hours later and several hundred dollars poorer," I complained.

"It is kind of amazing," my husband said.

"All I wanted was a few days away to do nothing," I whined. "Is that really so much to ask?"

"Apparently so," replied my husband. "Maybe we haven't learned to lower our expectations far enough yet."

"Does this mean we'll have to take some kind of course now?" I groaned.

"Nah, I have a better idea," he said, yawning.

"What?" I asked.

"Whenever we get the urge to go on a little vacation, we'll just take our money, put it in a pile and set fire to it," he said.

"Well, it certainly would be simpler."

"And after all," said my husband nodding off against my shoulder, "simpler is what it's all about."

Home safe and sound, my husband snoring gently next to me and the dog and child still confined to their respective kennels, I had a sudden craving for Van Camp's Baked Beans.

19

MOMENTS OF TRUTH

If there is any comfort to be found in approaching forty, it is knowing that I am not alone. In fact, I am in very good company. Figures drawn from the latest U.S. census reveal that approximately forty-six million American women are, at this very moment, poised on the brink of midlife. That fact can be interpreted two ways. On the one hand, it is exciting to think of the tremendous energy and potential released by forty-six million women entering a new phase of their lives. Women who have left the insecurity and uncertainty of their twenties and thirties in the dust. Women who have acquired the self-assurance, savvy, and personal freedom to boldly explore new vistas. Women who in many ways are being reborn as entirely different people. I get kind of tingly just writing the words.

On the other hand, forty-six million women entering midlife simultaneously does pose a bit of a safety hazard. I mean, let's face it, forty-six million midlife women — that's a lot of falling flesh. If by some weird cosmic coincidence — a kind of disharmonic convergence — all of that flesh crashes earthward at the same moment, the resulting shock waves could make the devastation wrought by history's worst earthquakes look like child's play. Thankfully, the chances of that happening are pretty slim. Even so, I'd guess that before the sun sets today, roughly 6,800 thighs, 4,200 upper arms, 12,000 breasts and a whopping 27,000 buttocks will all be hanging a lot closer to the ground than they were just yesterday. (Not to mention the corresponding number of egos they will take down with them.)

For many a midlife woman, a face-to-face encounter with her own falling flesh constitutes what I term a Moment of Truth, a moment of such clarity that there can be no denying its meaning: aging is running amok in her life. Still, the catalog of Moments of Truth contains a variety of experiences as deep, rich, and individualized as women themselves. For instance, the same woman who accepts the morphing of her upper arms into bat wings with quiet nonchalance may be shaken to the point of hysteria the day she realizes she needs arm (or wing, as the case may be) extensions in order to read price tags, fabric-care labels and telephone book entries. I'd like to share with you some of the Moments of Truth I have gathered from my friends, ostensibly so that we can all learn from each other's experiences, but in reality to ridicule their private foibles for mass entertainment. And, by the way, if you haven't had a Moment of Truth yet, well, all I can say is 1) we have absolutely nothing in common 2) I pretty much hate you, and 3) don't get too comfortable, honey, it's just a matter of time.

While the specifics vary from woman to woman, some general themes emerge when women begin discussing the question: "When did you first realize you were getting old?"

For instance, memory lapses — as documented by the following:

"Kathy" speaks: "I called one of my best friends at her

office. When the receptionist asked who I wanted to speak with, I couldn't remember my friend's name. I stuttered something about calling the wrong number to the — I'm guessing here — twenty-two-year-old with cellulite-free thighs on the other end of the line and hung up in humiliation. I felt so foolish."

"Donna" speaks: "I keep forgetting everyone's names. I mean everyone, including people I have known for years. I started to introduce two of my friends at a party and all of a sudden, I couldn't think of their names. I stammered around and ended up saying something like, 'Everybody, this is my friend, and this is my other friend.' It was horrifying."

"Elizabeth" speaks: "I have started forgetting my children. Not their names, but the fact that I have them. I have had ten years to get used to having them around, yet I keep misplacing them. I have left my son stranded at school and soccer practice several times this past year because I honestly forgot about him. I foresee very high therapy bills in this child's future."

"Lynn" speaks: "I was on the phone, interviewing a photographer I wanted to hire for a shoot in another city. In the middle of a sentence, I became distracted and forgot her name. Trying to think of her name made me lose my train of thought, and then while trying to recapture it, I just blanked out on everything and essentially fell apart. I said, 'I'm so sorry, I'm forty-two, and I have no idea who you are or what we're talking about.' She replied, 'I'm forty-three, and I'll tell you my name again if you'll tell me yours.'"

Another memory-related topic is the ever-popular "Putting Things in Inappropriate Places/Canned Sardines Do Not Belong in Your Jewelry Drawer" theme. Again, my friends tell their stories:

"Donna" speaks: "I have been eating breakfast for forty-two years; I should have the routine down by now. Suddenly, putting the milk and cereal away presents a challenge for me. Three times in the past few months, I have put the cereal in the refrigerator and the milk in the cupboard. I'm on to myself now, so I double-check, but the first time I made the switch, it turned out nasty. I put the milk in the cupboard and left for a three-day weekend. It was gross."

"Ann" speaks: "I went shopping the other day and bought a package of napkins. Yet, later when I went to get them out of the pantry where I always keep them, they weren't there. I looked everywhere and cursed the bag boy for putting my napkins in someone else's bag. Later that evening, I opened the dishwasher to load the dinner plates, and there were the napkins. It was scary."

"Elizabeth" speaks: "My husband said he is going to sew a tag on our dog that says 'Dry Cleaning Not Recommended.' The other day, I put the dog in the car to take her for her checkup. She was so quiet that I kind of forgot she was there, and I started thinking about other things. I guess at some level of consciousness it registered that I had a 'load' in the backseat, and I automatically pulled up to the drive-thru dry cleaners to drop it off. In my defense, they do claim to be 'Fur Specialists.'"

(As a side note, I was recently informed that aging makes it harder to hold onto more than just your memory. I was discussing an upcoming project with my boss, an incredibly capable, on-top-of-it woman, when I realized she had forgotten some small, critical details. "See," she said when I pointed out her uncharacteristic oversight, "I told you I can't remember anything anymore. I am becoming completely incompetent."

"Well, that's better than being completely incontinent," I said, trying to cheer her up.

She was quiet for a moment and then said flatly, "Oh. I haven't told you, have I?" The thought of sneezing in public now strikes terror in her heart!)

Another popular category of Moments of Truth is "So Who Asked Ya?/Rude and Stupid Remarks from Friends and Strangers." With the possible exception of pregnancy, no condition elicits uninvited commentary from complete strangers like women's aging does. Before I gave in to shading my hair, I had a woman pull me aside at a cosmetics counter and tell me confidentially that she thought I was "just so brave" to let my gray show. She was dead serious. I looked at her and said, "Brave? You really think this is brave?"

"Oh, indeed I do," she replied. "And you're out in public just as proud as you please. I say, 'good for you, you brave little soldier.'" She believed every word she was saying. It was pathetic.

"Let me explain something to you," I said. "Donating a kidney to a dying relative is brave. Throwing yourself on a live grenade is brave. Raising children in the '90s where influences like yours abound could even be construed as somewhat brave, but declining to color my hair is not an act of bravery."

She just looked at me blankly as if she hadn't heard a word and said, "Of course, I couldn't do it because of my image and everything." What could I say to that?

Children's comments, while more innocent, represent a whole new adventure in humiliation. My friend Pam used to work as a dental hygienist. One day the little boy in her chair, who had been staring intently at her face throughout the whole cleaning process, said very thoughtfully, "Miss Pam, you should iron your face, especially around your eyes. Then you wouldn't have all those wrinkly parts."

My daughter's first-grade teacher, who at thirty-six had a head of lustrous gray hair, once recounted to me this conversation she overheard in the cafeteria. One of her students said, "I think Mrs. Barnes is sixteen, but her hair is older, like maybe about a hundred." The other one replied authoritatively, "My mom says Mrs. Barnes is immaturely gray."

Then there's my friend Susan. "I knew I was old the day I looked down at myself in a bathing suit and realized someone had taken my thighs while I was asleep and replaced them with my mother's. Overnight I had developed midlife thighs, the ones covered with more red and blue lines than an accurately scaled map of the state of Wisconsin."

A few days after her startling discovery, Susan was standing in line at Dairy Queen when she overheard two twelve-year-old boys behind her talking about her legs. "Lookin' good," said one. "Really good," said the other. Susan chuckled softly to herself, maybe her midlife thighs weren't so bad afterall.

"You ask her," said Boy One.

"No, you," answered Boy Two.

"Okay, I will. Hey, lady where'd you get the cool tattoo?" asked Boy One with genuine admiration.

"Tattoo?" asked Susan.

"Yeah, that one on your thigh. The blue octopus," explained Boy One, fascinated.

"With extra red arms," Boy Two added. "Hey, are you in, like, a gang or something?"

Susan immediately exchanged her place in line at Dairy Queen for one at the Vein Clinics of America.

My friend, Marilee, suggests "Growth of Random Body Hair" for inclusion in the Moments of Truth Hall of Fame.

"You know you are getting old when it takes you longer to pluck your cheeks than to pluck your eyebrows," she told me last week, fuming with indignation. "Look," she said, "when I started finding gray eyebrow hairs, I went along with it. When the occasional chin hair cropped up, I tended to it without fanfare. I even agreed to tolerate a proliferation of nasal hair, should that someday be my cross to bear. But I am drawing the line at this!"

"You have cheek hair?" I asked, trying to clarify the parameters of this crisis.

"Cheek hair?" she bellowed. "I would be thrilled to have cheek hair. I have cheek tresses! These things are long, longer than my head hair. It took me so long to pluck them all, my hand cramped up. And now my face is all red and sore. What am I going to do?"

I suggested she pull her flowing facial tresses into a stylish updo, but she wasn't amused. In fact, her exact words were: "Pluck you, Lee." (She's so testy these days — another sure sign of aging.)

I can relate to all of my friends' Moments of Truth, but the incident that personally hit me the hardest occurred two years ago at a party. For some reason, we were all talking about where we were when various historic events had taken place. Naturally, the day JKF was killed was near the head of the list. Some people were at the dentist, some were in traffic, some were in college and some were in kindergarten. When it was my turn, I recalled how Sister Pierre Francis announced the shattering news over the PA system, and how two days later, my mother almost broke her leg running to the livingroom TV set — which had been on continuously since the day of the assassination — when the sound of Jack Ruby's gunshots rang out in the middle of our Sunday dinner.

We all stood in quiet reflection, sharing a moment of generational bonding when Beth turned to Sandy and asked, "What about you, Sandy? Where were you?"

"I couldn't really say," said Sandy noncommittally.

"You mean you don't remember?" Beth asked.

"Not exactly," Sandy replied, shifting from foot to foot.

"Oh, my gosh, you don't mean to say — " I started.

Beth guessed the rest. "You weren't born yet, were you?" she asked accusingly.

"Well, no, I wasn't. But I wish I had been, I really do," Sandy said apologetically.

"Yeah, well, you should have thought about that before you waited until 1965 to be conceived," Beth scolded her.

I couldn't quite get my mind around Sandy's revelation. How, I wondered, could it be possible for someone not to have been born when President Kennedy was killed. What kind of topsy-turvy world were we living in? Then Sandy made another shocking confession. She revealed that she, the one who had always referred to herself as being "about the same age as you guys" when she was among us, was actually still a few months shy of her thirtieth birthday. We couldn't believe she had been in her twenties, masquerading as a real person, the whole time we had known her. It was like being on a G-rated version of Jerry Springer. We didn't know how to think of her now. In the end, we decided we could still like her, but it would never be like it could have been if she had had the good sense to be born earlier. Fair is fair.

Still, I felt kind of sorry for her. It probably wasn't all her fault. No doubt her parents had something to do with her poorly timed conception. Blame the family of origin whenever possible, that's my thinking. "Don't take it so hard, Sandy," I consoled her. "Your generation, whatever that is, will have its own touchstones. Years from now, when people talk about the shock waves caused by the 'big one' of 1999

— you know, the day all of the boomer behinds hit the ground at the same time — you can impress all of the young people in the crowd by telling them you not only remember where you were when it happened, you knew some of those behinds personally."

She brightened considerably at that thought. "Yeah, that makes me feel better," she said and poured herself a glass of wine, which, after all, she was legally old enough to do. Sandy was going to make it. I was happy for her despite the way she had deceived us.

I was happy for myself, too. I had managed to put another person's comfort ahead of my own pride — a definite aging milestone and the silver lining in many a dark Moment of Truth.

20

DÉJÀ VOODOO

When my daughter's friends heard I was writing a book, they all begged to be in it. "Oh, please, Mrs. Potts, it would rule to have our names in it." Since they are such good kids, I'm obliging: Lauren, Courtney, Jodi and daughter Torrie, you are now in print! But their request points out one of the biggest problems with teenagers, namely that they have little use for logic. If they had given the matter any serious consideration at all, they would have realized that being included in my book would not necessarily be a good thing for them. I wanted to say, "Think this through, girls. I am writing a book about my midlife crisis, about the loss of my youth. What makes you think that I would paint teenagers, who represent everything I'm mourning the loss of and who are contributing greatly to my rapid deterioration, in a favorable light?" But they don't think that far beyond themselves. They're fifteen — they think the sun shines solely to show off the highlights in their hair.

And now that I've cracked the door on the subject of today's youth, I might as well fling it wide open and tell you what really bothers me. I know these words will indelibly inscribe my name in the official old person's registry, but I can't help myself: Why are these kids in such a hurry to grow up? The girls have a full set of gel nails by the time they're four and get their ears pierced in utero, for crying out loud! What's next, prenatal tummy tucks? The boys, on the other hand, wait until shortly after birth to get their earrings, but begin shaving before kindergarten. Forget milk mustaches, these little guys wake up from nap time with three o'clock shadows.

And moving right along, since when did it become customary for thirteen- and fourteen-year-olds to eat in regular, sit-down restaurants unchaperoned? When was that ordinance passed? I met my girlfriend for dinner at Chili's one night, and we had to wait more than an hour for a table because the place was crawling with unparented youths (mine probably among them), who had availed themselves of the phone-ahead wait list. Okay, my generation wasn't exactly about meeting Jughead at the Malt Shop, but McDonald's was still a pretty big deal for us. Reserved as a weekend treat, for sure. But, not for these kids. Last year my daughter, who was fourteen at the time, called to ask if she and her friends could go to Starbucks after school for — get this — a latte! Give me a break. What, the Slush Puppy machine at 7-Eleven was out of order?

But, my daughter has always had sophisticated tastes. When she was nine, we had this conversation:

HER: Mommy, I'd like to shop in France all day and then eat at a little café. (Which she pronounced simply "caf," without the accented "e.")

ME: (Giggling) Café?

HER: Well, café, caf, whatever, it would be lovely.

Everything is so much more advanced with kids nowadays. My daughter was only thirteen when she started hinting around to my husband and me that she thought she and her friends were old enough to go downtown to a concert by themselves. Hoping that sending us on a nostalgic trip down memory lane would make us more inclined to agree, she asked my husband to recall the first concert he ever attended. His time-warped answer? The Cowsills! With his parents! I had been silently praying that he'd have the good sense to say Up with People, but all the same, The Cowsills with his parents versus, say, Alice in Chains with other thirteen-year-olds, made our point pretty well. She went down in flames that round. (For the record, I wouldn't have given her permission to go downtown alone to see Alice in Wonderland, much less Alice in Chains!) I'm telling you, kids, think things through first.

I know it's tougher for kids today, but it's tougher for parents, too. For instance, I know that adolescent girls have been mooning over movie stars since Rudolph Valentino appeared in *The Sheik*, and I was certainly no different. I spent hours in my room, clutching a picture of the chosen hunk-of-the-week close to my heart and plotting out the minutest details of our future life together. But times have changed. Whereas my mother could relax when I was holed up with my *Tiger Beat* photos of Barry Williams, I have to patrol the borders of my daughter's life vigilantly, ready to intercept any stray copies of the Brad Pitt issue of *Playgirl* that might be trying to invade her territory. Thank goodness the judge ruled to recall the rest of the issues. (Although I understand one of the stylists at my hair salon snagged a copy. I, of course, haven't looked at it, but even if I had, it would be totally inappropriate for me to comment on it in this context. Wouldn't it?)

The freedom of high school, compared to middle school, has been dizzying to my daughter and her friends. After years of being strictly segregated by grade level, they now find themselves grouped in with junior and senior guys who treat them like . . . equals. (Equals, my foot. They're just scoping out the fresh crop of babes.) Every night brings another invitation to go somewhere. "On a school night?" I balk in provincial disbelief. And in the summer, every day brings another "last-chance" event that my daughter thinks merits a curfew extension. It's always a last time of some sort or other. There has been the last time they'll be together before Ryan leaves for a summer study program, before Josh leaves for the lake, before the girls leave for camp, and before the dog leaves for the vet to get her teeth cleaned.

It is ridiculous. They want to run wide open, full throttle from morning to night. (Just who is supposed to empty the dishwasher while they're out running all over the countryside is what I want to know.) I keep trying to get them to slow down, trying to convince them to save some excitement for the rest of their lives. "If you girls did everything you wanted now in high school — which would occur over my dead body, you understand — you'd have nothing left to look forward to later," I say to Torrie and Courtney, building my case.

"You mean, like if we could stay out late every night and all weekend long? Go to movies and concerts and out to eat everyday?" they ask.

"Something like that," I say.

"Wow, that would be awesome!" they marvel.

"Yes, but then you'd be tired of it by the time you graduated," I say. "Then what would you do?"

"Who cares?" they answer in unison. "That's three whole years away."

Oh, to be of an age when three years seemed longer than two blinks and a nod. In my head, I am screaming, "Three years is such a negligible amount of time, it is almost impossible to measure. It's barely a blip on the screen. I take naps that last longer than that!" But I save my words of wisdom for another day; my words won't — can't, actually — be heard by my fresh-faced audience right now. There is no way to convince fifteen-year-olds that their future — three whole years away — will be pulling into the station before they know it, and that they'll be scrambling to get on board.

Yet, even in the midst of discussions conducted from opposite corners of the universe, what seem most striking to me aren't the differences that exist between my daughter's generation and mine, but rather the similarities. Fifteen years into motherhood, and I still find myself thrown by the realization that I am now the parent and not the child. How is that possible? I feel like I fall through a crack in the invisible wall that separates the past from the present about a hundred times a day as I watch and listen to my daughter and her friends do and say all the things my friends and I did. The high-pitched squeals, the hair talk, the endless quoting of every single line from *Wayne's World*, (*Young Frankenstein*, in my case), the constant teetering back and forth between self-consciousness and self-confidence, all of it feels so real to me. And I remember it not as some distant half-memory, but as my contemporary experience.

At times these girls replay my life with such poignancy, with such authenticity, that my own youth becomes almost palpable, as if it is rising up from some secret hiding place to meet me. I instinctively reach out my hands, believing that if I can stretch just a little farther, my fingertips will brush against it once more. But, I never quite get there before it evaporates. The spell breaks, and I end up shaking my head, confounded by the idea that a mother and a daughter can be the very same age, at the very same time. How is that so? This is more than a simple case of déjà vu, I conclude; it's déjà voodoo.

Déjà voodoo ran rampant last summer during a weekend visit to Washington, D.C. Having been away from the area for several years, my husband and I headed to Georgetown to see if one of our favorite jazz clubs was still standing. Just being in Georgetown should have tipped me off that a déjà voodoo experience of the first order was imminent. You can't walk around that place for more than ten minutes without noticing that the shocking trend of admitting eleven-year-olds to college has gotten out of hand. "We looked so much older than these kids when we were in school," I insisted.

We got to the club, and it was wonderful — still very cool, very hip. I felt young again, exuberant, carefree even. I had a marvelous time all the way through the first set. Then the band broke, and I started looking around the room. I may have felt nineteen again, but these kids really were. And they were smoking, drinking, and oozing enough hormones to permanently alter the chemical composition of all life forms within a twenty-mile radius. I was afraid I would get pregnant if I breathed too deeply. In the back of the room, a swarm of boy-children was buzzing around this one girl-child who was wearing a little black spandex number the size of a cocktail napkin. I wanted to yell, "She's just a baby!" and shoo them away. (And throw a coat over her.) All I could see was the face of my own "baby" at home, who was herself not too many years away from being in a place just like this. (I made a mental note to begin calling convent schools in the morning.)

"This is outrageous! These beautiful, pink-lunged children are smoking!" I ranted. "We've got to do something."

"There's nothing we can do about it tonight," my husband said, trying to head me off at the pass.

"Speak for yourself," I told him. "I'm taking names and numbers."

"Honey, you can't stop them," he said calmly.

"Oh, so you think it's okay that they're smoking, drinking and . . . everything else-ing?"

"No, of course not. I just don't know what you can do about it right now," he answered.

"Plenty," I told him. "For starters, I can, well, I can . . . get upset about it, that's what I can do," I sputtered in frustration.

"And that will accomplish exactly what?" he asked.

"Oh, I can't believe you," I sniffed. "What if it were Torrie? Would you be so casual then? Or maybe that would be perfectly fine with you?" Even with my self-righteousness in high gear, I knew that was a ludicrous statement. I shot him a sheepish grin. "I'm sorry," I said. "I just can't stand to think of all the bad things that could happen to these kids. To any kids. To our kid."

"I know," he said. "Do you want to go?"

"No, I'm fine," I said. "I want to stay."

We did stay and had a great time. Of course every now and then, warnings like "Put out that cigarette right now, missy" and "Don't even think about doing that with her, buster" could be heard above the strains of a David Sandborn tune. At 2:30 A.M., my husband took my arm and led me to the door. "C'mon, Ms. Deputy Dog," he teased. "You've issued your last citation for the evening. It's time to go home."

We strolled down the street arm in arm. "Boy, that really took you back, being in there tonight, huh?" I said reflectively.

"Yes, it did," my husband agreed.

"That used to be us," I said.

"Déjà vu," he said.

"Except we were so much more mature than those kids.

And more responsible. And made much wiser fashion choices," I said.

"That's the way you remember it, huh?" he asked.

"Absolutely. I can see it all very clearly in my mind's eye," I said with mock assurance.

"I suspect that particular memory is more the result of déjà voodoo than déjà vu," he laughed. "But, at the ripe old age of thirty-nine, I know better than to argue with Deputy Dog," he said affectionately and squeezed me tightly about the waist. "But now it's my turn to give the orders. Assume the position, Baby," he said playfully, pulling me close to him. I detected some of my own hormones beginning to stir. We kissed under the streetlight before heading up the hill to our car.

Eat your hearts out, all you nineteen-year-olds! There are some things you're simply too young to appreciate.

21

THE PAST IMPERFECT

"Put down whatever you're thinking of eating because this twentieth high school reunion thing is going through," said my friend Ginny when I picked up the phone. I had just walked in the door from work and was at that very moment holding an English muffin, negotiating with myself for a little peanut butter. "I can eat both halves plain and an apple," I bargained. "Or one half plain and one half with jelly, no apple. Or one half with peanut butter, no other half, no apple." I really, really wanted the peanut butter. But the news of this cataclysmic event had suddenly altered my timetable for losing the four pounds that had found their way onto my hips via several strawberry daiquiris consumed on a sun-drenched vacation beach a few weeks earlier.

I recoiled at the thought of putting another morsel in my mouth for the next two weeks and threw down the English muffin as if it were radioactive. "Okay, if I limit myself to one rice cake or one styrofoam cup per day, my choice, and drink lots of water," I was saying when Ginny interrupted to drop the real bomb. "I know for a fact," she said, lowering her voice at least one octave, "that *he* is going to be there." "He," of course, referred to my old boyfriend whom I had not seen in several years. I grabbed a spoon and the whole jar of peanut butter. Shoot, this was no time for pretense. Let the rice cakes fall where they may. This was big. Really big. I needed sustenance.

So, he was going to be there. What did that mean to me? I hadn't taken the lid off that box of memories in a long time. I didn't know what it would be like to see him again. But I did know this: If I were going to see him, I had to look hot. I mean fry-an-egg-on-me hot because I had to redeem myself for the way I looked the last time he saw me, which was two days postpartum. (For me, that is, not him.)

Is that a woman's worst nightmare or what? I was in the hospital in Pennsylvania having a baby, he was supposed to be safely sequestered in medical school in New York, a full state away, when — surprise! — he turned up in the same hospital. With unrestricted access to my chart and all the gory details! (Thirty-eight pounds, any other questions?) There I was, having just blowed a whole in the thing, entertaining my old boyfriend in my hospital room. The only time in my life I had any cleavage at all, and I was rigged up in a nursing harness, the faint odor of sour milk my only perfume. Oh yeah, that was just the way I wanted him to remember me. As he left the room, his sigh of relief — as in "Thank God I didn't marry her" — was nearly audible. This was the image I had to come back from. A bit of a deficit as you can see.

Except for the peanut butter incident, I adhered to a strict styrofoam-and-water regimen for the two weeks preceding the reunion and hoped for the best. (There is a bubbly little waitress who regrets ever asking me if I was "saving room" for Piled High Heath Crunch Pie as she set down my meal of ice chips and club soda. As far as I'm concerned she got off easy. Some minor abrasions around her throat. Big deal. I was still packing 2.5 extra pounds one week before flight time.) At last, D-day arrived. The anticipation, the anxiety, the rice cakes, all were about to come to an end. I closed my eyes, took a deep breath and with hands and heart clenched, stepped into 1975 . . .

The curtain is rent. I'm crossing the threshold between the present and the past. A kaleidoscope of images and feelings. What year is this? Indeed, what lifetime is this? Different universes colliding and collapsing at once. Traversing great fissures in time with dizzying speed. A sea of faces surrounds me. Some recognizable, some not. There's Ginny, of course, and Gary and Timmy and, turning around, I see, oh my God, I see him. What do I feel? What do I think? Twenty years evaporate in a single turn of my head, and suddenly I am staring straight into the face of my youth. Looking into the eyes that first helped me to see myself. Who are you, you sweet and unfamiliar familiar face? It's like being in a house of mirrors, looking into his eyes and seeing myself reflected there. Isn't it funny, I think, that it is impossible for any of us to look at ourselves directly; we must trust the reflection we see in the mirror to show us, to a large degree, who we are. And looking at you now, these many years later, I wonder, my dear unfamiliar familiar face, my earliest of mirrors, who did you show me to be back then? Many times I believe it was someone much better and kinder and wiser than I actually was. Many times I believe you reflected not who I was, but who I would be. Who I believe I have now become, the disparate strands of my life finally twisting into a single thread. A thread that ties me securely to the richness of the present even as it gently binds me to the sweetness of the past. Oh, but I did love you so.

These are the deep and complex thoughts that were

spinning endlessly in my head. Thoughts that, when I opened my mouth to speak, were cleverly framed as "So, where do you live? How many kids do you have? And how are your parents?" ("Oh, your parents are fine?" I was tempted to respond, as the thought of them jolted me out of my dreamy reverie and into reality. "Gee, I'm sorry to hear that. I was so hoping they had contracted a rare flesh-eating disease that had left both of them hideously disfigured and shunned by society." Hey, I have my reasons. In my life, there has been maybe one person who held me in lower esteem than his parents did. A news director in West Virginia, but he was the anti-Christ and therefore not too well-regarded himself, so I don't think he even really counts.

So, what did I really want to ask? Well, I wanted to ask if he remembered the time he let me set his hair with hot curlers and put makeup on him. I wanted to ask if he remembered the time we made up words to "Rhinestone Cowboy" and sang into the tape recorder like a really bad country duo, though we declared ourselves to be "right good singers." I wanted to ask if when he saw an Irish setter he ever heard my voice in his head saying, "That's the kind of dog we are going to have someday when we don't get married." (Phraseology used in deference to his fear of entrapment.) I wanted to ask if he would do me the supreme favor of forgetting all the junk and remembering only the good stuff. I have, and that's no small accomplishment, considering I have every minor event in my life mentally cross-referenced by date, place, and color of underwear I was wearing at the time.

And I would have said that I am happy and whole. I would have said I have married the most remarkable man. A man who loves me with an irrational extravagance. Who does not simply tolerate my excesses, but celebrates them. A man who says the greatest joy in his life is watching me inhabit mine so fully. Who honestly believes, though God only knows why, that I hung the moon. A man who needs me to pull him out of this world as much as I need him to pull me back into it. A man who tells me quite firmly "You are fine" while I'm awaiting a biopsy report, and who reaches for me in his sleep, sobbing with relief, "You are fine" after the results have come back as he predicted. A man whose shedding season knows no bounds and whose idea of washing his face involves hurling a gallon of water against the wall and catching whatever splashes off head-on. Or so it would appear from the counter on his side of the bathroom. This is the man I married.

I would have said that I have friends who love and care for me in the most tender of ways. Friends who have held my hand and prayed for me when I could not form the words. Friends who have given me their strength and faith when I could muster none of my own. Friends who cause me to spit Diet Coke halfway across a restaurant because we laugh so much when we are together. Friends who think I am the spark, the light, the featured attraction in their lives. Who think, in their words, "Lee is the party." They've got it wrong, though, they are the party, and I am honored to be attending.

I would have said that I am the mother of the neatest kid in the world. She is beautiful, sweet, quick and frightfully insightful. "Mom," she said during my postreunion melancholy, "if you let the past make you sad, then you'll be sad all the time because the past is happening every minute. What I am saying right now is the past as soon as I finish saying it. You have to learn to live with the past because there is an awful lot of it around." Somewhere in there is a profound thought, and I told her as much. "Well," she replied smiling, "I want to be a child psychologist, and since you have the mind of a child I can psychologize you."

And, finally, just for good measure, I would have told him that I have never forgotten the way he smelled back then. The sweet smell of a baby, a heady fragrance indeed, can make me woozy, but the smell of a high school boy, a magical elixir of soap and shaving cream, anticipation and promise, is completely intoxicating.

That's what I would have said.

— Conclusion —

IMPONDERABLES AND THE SECRET OF LIFE

When I was a new mother I used to wake up in the middle of the night in a cold sweat, my heart pounding, a feeling of total panic enveloping me. "What's wrong?" my husband would ask frantically. I would then dissolve into tears, barely able to stammer out the source of my terror. "Do you realize that someday our baby will be . . . ten! Oh, think of it, ten years old. She was just a baby, how could she be ten already?" Wails and mournful cries of despair echoing through the night. Every fear imaginable taking shape in the darkness. "What if I'm not a good mother? What if I ruin her life? What if she hates me by the time she's ten?" (My husband, ever supportive, told me I didn't have to wait that long for someone to hate me. He'd oblige me right then if I didn't stop being ridiculous and go to sleep!)

Well, we made it through age ten and just rounded the bend on fifteen, and to my knowledge, my daughter has not yet publicly renounced me. (She has asked me to not get out of the car on a few occasions, but I believe that falls within the accepted parent-child embarrassment parameters, considering I was wearing red sweat pants with stretched-out elastic, white flip-flops and a ponytail. It was a dress-down Friday.) Still, the midnight fears stalk from time to time. And the older I get, the bolder the fears and questions get. They have bled well beyond the borders of child care into other sensitive areas. And they stage assaults in broad daylight, shamelessly interrupting my routine. In fact, it is sometimes hard for me to finish more than one load of laundry in a day without having to stop to battle life's tough questions.

Riddled with self-doubt and recrimination at having missed putting the Downy in the final rinse cycle yet again (can I do nothing right?), I lean against the washer and stare down the black, menacing questions that, if we are honest, haunt us all in quiet moments. Questions like "What if I only think I know the truth about myself? What if, in fact, every important decision I have ever made is wrong? What if all my actions are the result only of my compulsive, unconscious need, thrusting me headlong into certain emotional disaster?" And, when I'm completely in the clutches of my dark side, I even allow, God forgive me, this blasphemous thought to be given voice: "If Martha Stewart has never eaten macaroni & cheese directly out of the pot with a wooden spoon while watching a 'Partridge Family' rerun, how much could she really know about living?"

There are so many hard questions. We shed blood, sweat, and tears, gnashing our teeth and railing against the injustice and difficulty of this life. We lose sleep, lose hair, and nearly lose our minds wrestling in the dark with tough choices and unsolvable problems. (And that's just regarding basic living issues. Forget sifting through cosmetic surgery options.) Following are a few of the thornier questions I've made a kind of peace with. Maybe they will help you.

Q: Is it possible to "have it all?"
A: No.

Q: Can you go home again?
A: That's a tough one because you must consider what you mean by "home." If by "home" you mean a city serviced by a major air carrier, it is possible, perhaps even at a substantial discount, provided you book fourteen days in advance and stay over a Saturday night. If, however, you mean something more metaphorical, say a period in time more than a geographic location, the answer is no. In short, while it is possible to go from Atlanta to Pittsburgh, it is not possible to go from age thirty-nine to age twenty-two. You can't get there from here.

Q: Is it unrealistic to think that we might someday live our lives from a perspective of love rather than fear?
A: Totally unrealistic.

Q: Is there any personal humiliation beyond having my husband tell a roomful of strangers how I lost control of my bowels during labor?
A: No. That's pretty much the outer limits.

Q: Can this same man ever find me attractive after having witnessed such an event?
A: Amazingly, yes. (He insists even more so, but men will say anything.)

Q: What are the most important qualities in a friend?
A: I'm glad you asked. People are often blinded by the obvious things — loyalty, thoughtfulness, honesty — and are lured into destructive relationships. Two issues that give the

clearest insight into a person's character are lighting usage and furniture placement. I once had a woman acquaintance who seemed too good to be true — funny, bright, interested in my welfare. And then I saw her apartment. She had zero undersanding of indirect lighting. I mean, the woman had overhead lights! Throughout her entire apartment! And she had furniture in the most obvious places. Like against walls. Not a shred of imagination or illusion to be found. This woman was clearly comfortable facing reality, and that is no basis for a friendship.

Q: Will I ever be comfortable living in the tension that exists between being an individual and being part of the group?
A: No chance.

Q: I heard a woman say that getting older keeps her focused on becoming "the best me I can be." How do you feel about this?
A: "The best me I can be?" Oh, please. Not without the liberal use of heavy-gauge wire and duct tape.

Q: How much Healthy Choice ice cream can you consume before it's no longer a healthy choice?
A: Conservatively speaking, I'd say at least a half-gallon, if you follow carefully prescribed rituals, such as eating directly out of the carton and eating all the melted stuff around the edges first. (It's permissible to use a microwave to speed the melting process if you're running late for an important appointment, say your feng shui consultant)

Q: What do women want?
A: Accessories, mainly. Both personal and for the home.

Q: What do women find most attractive in men?
A: The party line: sensitivity. The atavistic truth: strength. The bare minimum: a job.

Q: Do orange M&M's contain beta-carotene?
A: Yes. I'm convinced they are an excellent source of this important nutrient, a fact that has been largely suppressed by both the popular press and the medical establishment, owing mainly to their long-standing bias against premenstrual women.

Q: Will driving down the highway on a warm Friday evening with all the windows down, blasting the Commodore's "Brick House" ("36-24-36, what a winning hand") on the radio cause permanent dementia?
A: The order is wrong here. That's not the cause of dementia, that's the effect. Actually, it is a soul-cleansing experience of the highest order. One that sure enough could knock a strong man to his knees . . . cause she's a brick house, she's mighty mighty, just letting it all hang out . . . she's a brick — oh, sorry.

Q: Can I achieve a graceful balance between maintaining high standards and becoming judgmental and restrictive?
A: Good luck.

Q: Is cellulite impervious to spiritual intervention?
A: Apparently so.

Q: What is the most important development of the twentieth century?
A: I'd have to go with acrylic nails on this.

Q: What if I'm not nearly as altruistic and compassionate as I like to think I am?
A: You're not, get over it. (Most of us would pick easy, pretty and nice over hard, ugly and mean if given a choice.)

As for all the other questions, well, some days I know the answers and some days I keep my head down at my desk, hoping the teacher won't call on me. If I am lucky, I'll have a few more years to keep studying. And I have to admit that as shocking as the idea of aging still is to me, I am beginning to see some good things about not being twenty years old anymore. For instance, the chances that I will have to live down the infamy of belting out "Beast of Burden" in a white halter dress from high atop a barstool are dramatically lower now. Likewise the chances that I will make myself sick consuming a breakfast of potato salad and raw cookie dough have diminished . . . well, somewhat. Despite all my whining, getting older is not quite as awful as I feared. In the end, an exchange of buns of steel for a more tender heart strikes me as a pretty good deal.

And now, dear reader, we have come to the end of our time together. I would like to offer this final insight by way of thanking you for indulging me on this journey across the years. Remember, when all is said and done, what's most important in life boils down to these three simple things: Relationship with God, community with man, and . . .

. . . like, really good jewelry.

Good luck and God bless.